Teacher's **2A** **Guide**

Apple Pie
Delta's Beginning ESL Program

Sadae Iwataki, Editor
Jean Owensby
Constance Turner
Greta Kojima

REVISED EDITION

© 1993 by Delta Systems Co., Inc.
Revised Edition 1995

ISBN 0–937354–62–7

Delta Systems Co., Inc.
1400 Miller Parkway
McHenry, IL 60050 U.S.A.

Apple Pie 2A
Table of Contents

Delta's Apple Pie, Teacher's Guide 2A

To the Teacher

Thank you for choosing Delta's **Apple Pie** as your ESL textbook. This series brings to you a comprehensive, carefully structured, realistically paced curriculum for the "beginning low" and "beginning high" levels, as defined by California's English as a Second Language Model Standards for Adult Education Program, in four books: student book 1A and 1B for beginning low ESL and student books 2A and 2B for beginning high ESL. It is appropriate for adult and young adult learners in the United States and abroad. Its content and structure were developed over many years of use in the adult ESL programs of the Los Angeles Unified School District.

The following is a brief overview of the lesson structure of **Apple Pie**, and general directions for using the teaching notes in this guide.

Something New: Every lesson begins with this oral introduction of new material through use of visuals to accompany a listening comprehension selection. The target vocabulary and structures are introduced without the textbook through a series of steps: listen only, comprehension check, listen and repeat, listen and respond.

Let's Talk: This is a dialogue that incorporates the new language in the meaningful context of a dialogue set in a real–life situation. Students first master the dialogue orally with the help of a dialogue visual, then practice it with and without the teacher's help, and finally practice it with a partner and /or say it aloud from memory.

Practice, Interaction, Practice Activity: These are sections that expand on the language presented in the previous sections by using it again in mini–dialogues for pair practice, situations for role plays, group activities, and mixers. The practice sections move from more controlled oral work to more open–ended or personalized oral practice.

Reading: Reading passages are related to the lesson topic, using similar structures and vocabulary to present new information. They are followed by discussion questions, which generally end with a reference to students' own thoughts or experiences.

Writing: The writing sections provide review and reinforcement while giving students a chance to practice spelling and punctuation. In books 2A and 2B, some lessons have sections called *More Writing*, which provide prompts for controlled or original writing of sentences and short paragraphs.

After the core lesson, it is important to continue using the new language by including the ***Review*** and ***Activity Pages*** in subsequent class sessions. This way students have many opportunities to internalize new structures and functions and use them in their everyday interactions in English. The *Activity Pages* may include focused listening exercises, "information gap" activities, games, mixers, reading and discussion of true stories, and other tasks that integrate the language skills in a variety of relevant, interesting interaction and skill–building activities.

After each of the eight units of three related lessons, there is an *Evaluation*, with Listening Comprehension, Reading, and Writing sections. This regular evaluation is meant to be done individually and then corrected to give students an indication of their progress and teachers an indication of the current needs of the class.

An essential element in the pedagogy of **Apple Pie** is the use of the hand–held visuals available for each book. These contain the illustrations for the *Something New* and *Let's Talk* sections of the lessons, and are used to teach new vocabulary, structures, and functions with aural and visual cues for understanding. On the back of each visual are the phrases, sentences, or dialogue to be presented, to that the new language can be introduced as students listen without looking at the textbook.

The *Let's Talk* and *Reading* sections, focused listening sections of the *Activity Pages*, and Listening Comprehension sections of the *Evaluations* also appear on the **Apple Pie Cassette** available to accompany each book. Instructions are given in this teacher's guide for presenting those sections by using the cassette to provide opportunities for students to develop better listening skills by hearing different voices, by hearing new material before they read it, and by doing listening exercises that require them to glean information to carry out a task.

Guide to symbols used in the teacher's guide:

 The "closed book" symbol is a reminder that this is an oral section of the presentation, during which students are not yet looking at their books.

 This symbol means "now open your books" and indicates that students are about to see in print the items that they have been practicing orally.

 This group symbol indicates that students will be moving around the room in an interaction that requires them to speak to several students, or that they will be participating in a group activity.

 A cassette symbol in the heading means that a section is recorded on the tape, allowing an alternative presentation of the section by having students listen to a dialogue, listen while reading a passage, or listen and pick out specific information in a focused listening exercise.

At the beginning of each lesson in the teacher's guide, you will find Communication Objectives for the lesson, new structures that appear in the lesson, and a list of the visuals and other instructional aids needed for presenting the lesson to your class.

Good luck and success to you all. We hope that the **Apple Pie** program will serve you well, and that your students will find learning English our way to be effective, confidence–building and fun!

Lesson 1

A Healthy Diet

Communication Objectives:
Identify various breakfast foods
Ask about and discuss preferences
Use a food pyramid to assess a healthy diet

New Structures:
Imperatives
Simple present
Negative *anything*

Visuals:

V1	coffee and doughnuts
V2	cereal, banana, bran muffin, and milk
V3	orange juice, eggs, bacon, hash–browned potatoes, toast, coffee
V4	grapefruit, pancakes, ham, coffee
V5	Let's Talk: Eat Some Breakfast
V6	The Food Pyramid

Other instructional aids: Pictures of foods from magazines, play food, or real food

Page 2

Opening: Greeting Old and New Friends

1. Explain difference between greeting old friends and meeting new ones for the first time.

2. Walk around the classroom, giving examples of both.

3. Have students do this, too. If possible, find two students who already know each other and demonstrate the first example.

4. Then find two students who do not know each other, and demonstrate the second example.

 5. Have all students walk around the room, practicing both examples, and substituting their own names.

Something New: What's for Breakfast?

1. Briefly explain lesson objective: To discuss and follow a healthy diet. Be sure students understand that a "diet" is not solely used in the phrase "go on a diet," but refers to a daily eating pattern.

2. Have students listen as you ask "What's for breakfast?" Hold up V1, and say "coffee and doughnuts."

3. Show V1 and have students repeat "coffee and doughnuts."

4. Ask again "What's for breakfast?" Show V1 and have students respond "coffee and doughnuts."

5. Repeat above steps with V2, V3, and V4.

☛ Practice: "What's your favorite breakfast?"

1. Explain meaning of *favorite* and give examples for yourself. Tell your favorite breakfast.

2. Have students practice the dialogues in the text.

3. Explain meaning of *just* in #2.

4. Point out the difference between information questions with *what* and yes/no questions with *do/does*.

📼 Let's Talk: Eat Some Breakfast*

1. Show V5 to establish the context of the conversation. Explain that Luisa, a teenager, is in a hurry to get to school, but that her mother wants her to eat breakfast first.

2. Model the dialogue as students listen, indicating the speakers by pointing to the visual or other means.

3. Model the dialogue again.

4. Model the dialogue and have class repeat.

5. Take one role and have class take the other role; then change roles.

6. Divide the class in half and have them take the two roles; then have them switch roles.

7. Have volunteers say the dialogue for the class.

Delta's Apple Pie, Teacher's Guide 2A

8. Have class open books and practice the dialogue in pairs.

* Cassette users can have the students listen to the dialogue first with books closed.

Discussion

1. Facilitate a discussion about the importance of good breakfasts, using questions #1–5 as a guide. Use visuals from the lesson or other pictures as samples.

2. Write some of students' ideas on the board.

Page 5

☛ Practice: "I can't, I'm late"

1. Have pairs of students practice dialogues with responses in text, and then their own responses.

2. Students can use the visuals from the lesson to substitute for the examples in this Practice.

☛ Practice Activity: What do you have for breakfast?

1. Explain that students will be walking around asking four different class-mates about what they eat and drink for breakfast.

2. Do the activity first as an example, walking around the room asking four students; then record their answers on the chart provided (or on the chalkboard).

 3. Have students do the activity. Walk around to monitor and help.

Page 6

Something New: Foods for a Healthy Diet

 1. Put food pyramid on chalkboard, show on overhead, or hold up V6.

2. Explain and give examples of foods from each food group, using the pictures or realia. Elicit other foods in each group from the students.

3. Give examples of a meal, using foods from each group.

 4. Have students open books and study the food pyramid.

5. Facilitate a discussion of a healthy diet, using questions #1–4 as a guide.

Page 7

☛ Practice Activity

1. Have pairs, groups, or individuals generate a list of foods in each group. Encourage them to name foods from their countries.

2. Make a list on the board of all the foods they come up with, including the foods from their countries.

Page 8   ☞ **Practice: "Is that a healthy breakfast?"**

1. Have pairs of students practice the dialogues with responses in the text, and then their own responses.

2. Students can use foods from the pyramid to substitute for the examples in this Practice.

📼 **Reading:** A Good Diet*

1. Read the passage to the class as students follow along in their books.

2. Check comprehension by asking oral questions about the passage.

3. Have students read the passage on their own.

*Cassette users can have students listen to the Reading first with books closed, and then listen again and read along silently.

Page 9   *Discussion*

Facilitate a discussion of a good diet using the questions as a guide.

✍ **Writing**

1. Have students write their own answers.

2. Circulate to check their work, or have pairs check each other's work.

3. Have individuals report their answers to the class.

Page 10   ✍✍ **More Writing**

1. Have students write down all the foods they ate yesterday.

2. Have them write those same items on the chart on page 10. Explain that they must decide which column to put each food in.

3. Have students tell you which list has the most items and if that's good or bad. Use expressions like *I think it's good because...*, or *It's bad because...*

4. Have pairs compare their charts to follow up.

Delta's Apple Pie, Teacher's Guide 2A

Lesson 1 Activity Page

Page 11 **A. Listen and check the food groups you hear.***

1. Write the three categories on the chalkboard. Explain that students will listen to people talking about their meals and that they need to put a check under the correct label for each food group they hear. Do the first one as an example.

2. Read script or play the tape. Then correct together.

   Script:
   1. I like to eat yogurt for breakfast. I put a little cereal on top and a strawberry or two.

   2. I usually eat half a grapefruit, a muffin and an egg for breakfast.

   3. I like to eat a cheese sandwich for lunch, and I usually drink a glass of apple juice.

   4. At 9:00 at night I get very hungry. Usually I go into the kitchen and take an apple and cheese, some crackers and a glass of milk. But I really want chocolate cake!

   5. I ate a very big lunch today. First I had tomato soup with some crackers. Next I had a small chef's salad with turkey and cheese. After that I had a fruit cup with some ice cream. Everything was delicious.

   6. I love to cook. Soup is my specialty. Here's my recipe. First I put in a chicken, then a couple of onions, a carrot, and some cabbage. Next I put in some rice. When it's almost finished I put in a half cup of sour cream and stir it around. Mmmmm. My family loves it!

*Cassette users can have students listen to the script on tape.

B. Read the meals below.

Have students fill out the chart and discuss their reasons with a partner.

Light Meals, Heavy Meals

Communication Objectives:

> Talk about meals and snacks
> Extend an invitation
> Accept/refuse an invitation

New Structures:

> *Would like* + noun
> *Would like* + verb
> Contrast of *Do you like* and *Would you like*

Visuals:

V7	a light breakfast
V8	a heavy breakfast
V9	a light lunch
V10	a heavy lunch
V11	a light dinner
V12	a heavy dinner
V13	Let's Talk: Are You on a Diet?
V14	popcorn
V15	potato chips
V16	a candy bar
V17	cookies
V18	a piece of pie
V19	nuts
V20	an apple
V21	a soft drink
V22	an ice cream cone

Other instructional aids: Pictures of foods, for both light and heavy meals

Page 12

✔ Review: A Good Diet

1. Show V6 (a food pyramid) and briefly review the significance of the pyramid.

2. Write on the chalkboard some foods that fall into each category on the pyramid.

3. Have the class discuss which foods they like and dislike.

Something New: Three Meals a Day

1. Briefly explain lesson objective: To talk about meals and eating habits.

2. Have students listen as you say "It's a light breakfast." Hold up V7.

3. Show V7 and have students repeat "It's a light breakfast."

4. Show V8 and say "It's a heavy breakfast."

5. Show V8 and have students repeat "It's a heavy breakfast."

6. Continue in this manner with V9, V10, V11 and V12.

7. Show V7, V9, V11 (light meals) and elicit correct responses.

8. Show V8, V10, V12 (heavy meals) and elicit correct responses.

Page 13 ☛ **Practice: "Are you a big eater?"**

1. Explain "big eater."

2. Have students practice the conversations in the text.

3. Students can reverse answers from negative to affirmative, and from affirmative to negative.

Let's Talk: Are You on a Diet?*

1. Show V13 to establish the context of the conversation: Sara is at work. It's lunchtime and her co–worker invites her for a hamburger.

2. Model the dialogue as students listen, indicating the speakers by pointing to the visual or other means.

3. Model the dialogue again.

4. Model the dialogue and have class repeat.

5. Take one role and have class take other role; then change roles.

6. Divide class in half and have them take the two roles; then have them switch roles.

7. Have volunteers say the dialogue for the class.

8. Have class open books and practice the dialogues in pairs.

*Cassette users can have students listen to the dialogue first with books closed.

Page 14

☞ Practice: "What's for lunch?"

1. Have students practice the two conversations in pairs.

2. Students can substitute any kind of "diet" type foods for the examples given.

3. Explain that *have a meal* and *having a meal* are the same.

4. Be sure students understand *I'd love to*.

5. Practice other types of invitations using *Would you like…?*

Something New: Snacks

1. Explain what a "snack" is.

2. Show V14–V22 one at a time. Say each item, repeat it, and have class repeat each item.

3. Vary the order in which you show the visuals, and elicit correct responses.

4. Have students open their books and repeat the items they have been practicing.

5. Read, or have a volunteer read the three questions. Then have volunteers answer orally.

Page 15

★ Something Extra: What Do You Like/What Would You Like Now?

1. Explain that *What do you like?* means in general, and that *What would you like?* means "What do you want now?"

2. Practice the dialogue as in the previous Let's Talk.

Page 16

☞ Practice: "I'd like some water"

1. Practice the dialogues as in the previous Practices.

2. Be sure students understand the difference between *I'd love it* and *I'd love to* from earlier in the lesson.

📼 Reading: American Coffee Shops*

1. Read the passage to the class as students follow along in their books.

2. Check comprehension by asking oral questions about the passage.

3. Have students read the passage on their own.

*Cassette users can have students listen to the Reading first with books closed, and then listen again and read along silently.

Discussion

Facilitate a discussion of coffee shops using the questions as a guide.

Page 17 ✍ **Writing**

1. Read the questions for the class. Explain the meaning of *prefer* and *preferences*.

2. Have students write the answers for themselves, except for #3, which tells their classmate's preferences.

3. Have 3 volunteers list their favorite foods on the chalkboard (1 student for each meal).

Lesson 2 Activity Pages

Page 18 **A. Listen to the meals and check light or heavy.***

Do the first one as an example. Then have students listen and do the rest.

Script:

1. I'd like a bowl of soup and some crackers please.

2. May I have a hamburger with cheese, french fries, cole slaw, a large coke and a large ice cream cone?

3. I want a potato. That's all, just a nice baked potato.

4. Let's see…what can I have for lunch? I can't eat french fries, too much oil, and too much salt, and I don't think I want a salad. I know, I want a cheese sandwich and a glass of tomato juice. That sounds perfect.

5. Would you pass me the chicken? Some salad? Of course, I love salad. Oh, and I'll have some of that rice, too! Are those green beans? Yes? I'd love a few of those. Delicious! What are we having for dessert? Apple pie? Mmmmmm. A big piece, please!

*Cassette users can have students listen to the script on tape.

B. Write a new menu.

      1. Have students follow the directions to write a less fattening meal for Sara.

      2. Discuss answers.

C. Write the missing words.

      1. Explain that students will choose from the words in the box to fill in the story about Sara.

      2. Correct on chalkboard or overhead transparency.

D. Work in a group. Ask and answer the questions.

      1. Demonstrate by asking one student his/her "favorite" for all seven items on the chart.

 2. Have students walk around and ask six students the same questions.

E. Work in a group. Look at your group's answers for exercise D, and plan a dinner menu for your group.

 Groups of 4–5 students will plan a dinner menu based on the members' food preferences from exercise D above.

Eating Out

Communication Objectives:
Order/serve food
Tell server how you want food prepared
Discuss tasks to prepare for a party

New Structures:
Questions with *how*

Visuals:

V23	scrambled
V24	over easy
V25	sunny side up
V26	rare
V27	medium rare
V28	well done
V29	black
V30	with sugar
V31	with cream and sugar
V32	plain
V33	with lemon
V34	with milk and sugar
V35	Let's Talk: How Would You Like Your Steak?

Page 22

✔ Review: Eating Habits

Your Daily Diet
Discuss what students like to eat for each meal.

Snacks
1. Elicit some snacks from class.

2. List students' answers and choose favorite snacks.

Something New: Ordering Food

1. Briefly explain the lesson objective: To order food in a restaurant and tell how you want it prepared.

2. Explain that there are a few ways to have eggs prepared.

3. Have students listen as you say "scrambled." Hold up V23

4. Show V23 and have students repeat "scrambled."

5. Repeat with V24 and V25.

6. Explain that there are a few ways to have meat prepared.

7. Have students listen as you say "rare." Hold up V26.

8. Show V26 and have students repeat "rare."

9. Repeat with V27 and V28.

10. Explain that there are a few ways to drink coffee.

11. Have students listen as you say "black." Hold up V29.

12. Show V29 and have students repeat "black."

13. Repeat with V30 and V31.

14. Follow the same process with tea, using visuals V32, V33, and V34

15. Quickly review all the visuals above.

Let's Talk: How Would You Like Your Steak?*

Page 23

1. Show V35 to establish the context of the conversation: Sara and Tomas are having an anniversary dinner at a restaurant. The waiter is taking their order.

2. Model the dialogue as students listen, indicating the speakers by pointing to the visual or other means.

3. Model the dialogue again.

4. Model the dialogue and have class repeat.

5. Take one role and have class take the other role; then change roles.

6. Divide the class in half and have them take the two roles; then have them switch roles.

7. Have volunteers say the dialogue for the class.

8. Have class open books and practice the dialogue in pairs.

*Cassette users can have the students listen to the dialogue first with books closed.

Page 24
☛ Practice: "I'd like it well done"

1. Explain the difference between *How would you like* something prepared (now) vs. *How do you like* it (generally).

2. Have students practice the dialogues in pairs.

🔊 Reading: A Potluck Party*

1. Explain concept of a potluck party.

2. Have students follow along as you read the story aloud.

3. Check comprehension by asking oral questions.

*Cassette users can have students listen to the Reading first with books closed, and then listen again and read along silently.

Page 25
Discussion

1. Have students look at the list of pre–party tasks.

2. Using the chart, discuss who needs to do each task.

3. Facilitate a discussion of potluck parties using questions #2–4 as a guide.

☛ Practice activity: Do you like eggs?

1. Put sample questions on the chalkboard and elicit appropriate responses.

 2. Have students go around the classroom asking others about food likes.

✍ Writing

1. This can be done for homework.

2. The next day, have volunteers read their stories for the class.

Page 26 **A. Listen to the order. Circle the correct information on the menu pad.***

    1. Explain that students will circle each food item they hear in each of the three orders.

    2. Read script or play the tape.

Script:

1. I'd like a steak sandwich, medium, with the salad. My wife wants the chicken sandwich. She'll have a small cola and I'll have a large lemon–lime soda. We both want coffee, no cream or sugar, after lunch.

2. My daughter would like the hamburger, well done, french fries and a small orange soda. My son will have the chicken sandwich and a large lemon–lime. As for me…hmmm, I'll try your steak sandwich, rare, with the salad and I'd like coffee with cream also.

3. Let's see…what do we want? Not sure, not sure. Oh, let's have a hamburger, well done, a chicken sandwich, oh, and let's get a steak sandwich, too. I like my steak well done. A large cola and a black coffee. And what will you have, dear?

*Cassette users can have students listen to the script on tape.

Page 27 **B. Walk around the classroom and find someone who...**

    1. Do the first two as an example.

     2. Have students walk around and complete the exercise. Be sure they have the names of six different students.

C. Make three sentences from the information you have.

    Students choose three of the six answers from Exercise B to write complete sentences.

Unit One **Evaluation**

Page 29 ### I. Listening Comprehension*

      1. Go over the directions for Part I with students.

      2. Read each item of the script two times, at normal conversational speed.

              Script:
              1. A healthy breakfast.

              2. I like my eggs sunny side up.

              3. He's on a diet.

              4. He likes his coffee with sugar.

              5. Are you on a diet?

              6. Is this a light lunch?

              7. They belong to the grain group.

      *Cassette users can have students listen to the script on the tape.

Page 30 ### II. Reading and III. Writing

      1. Go over the directions for Parts II and III with students.

      2. Have class do these sections independently.

Evaluation Check

      1. Correct evaluation by having student volunteers write their answers on the board or an overhead transparency.

      2. Have class check their answers.

      3. Circulate to make sure students have checked their work accurately.

Postal Services

Communication Objectives:
Discuss post office services
Follow mailing instructions
Write a friendly letter

New Structures:
None

Visuals:

V36	First Class mail for the U.S. costs 32 cents.
V37	A postcard for the U.S. costs 20 cents.
V38	A First Class stamp for Mexico costs 35 cents.
V39	International airmail costs 50 cents.
V40	An aerogram for international mail costs 45 cents.
V41	Let's Talk: First Class Mail Goes by Air
V42	Parcel Post (4–10 days)
V43	Express Mail (overnight)
V44	Priority Mail (2–3 days)

Other instructional aids: Realia from post office, including several denominations of stamps, aerogram, envelope, tape, tissue, padding, etc.

Page 32

✔ Review: Eating Out

1. Have half the class role play server/customer in a coffee shop for breakfast.

2. Have the other half of the class role play server/customers in a restaurant for a special occasion.

Something New: Postal Services

 1. Briefly explain the lesson objective: To use postal services.

2. Explain that there are five kinds of letter–mail that you can send.

3. Hold up V36 and say "First Class mail for the U.S."

4. Show V36 and have students repeat "First Class mail for the U.S."

5. Repeat the process for the other visuals, V37, V38, V39, V40.

6. Repeat all five visuals and have students repeat.

Discussion

Page 33

Facilitate a discussion of different kinds of mail, using questions #1–4 as a guide. Talk about price and purpose of each kind of mail.

Let's Talk: First Class Mail Goes by Air*

Page 34

1. Show V41 to establish the context of the conversation: Tranh wants to send two letters, one to Mexico City and one to Seattle, WA.

2. Model the dialogue as students listen, indicating the speakers by pointing to the visual or other means.

3. Model the dialogue again.

4. Model the dialogue and have class repeat.

5. Take one role and have class take the other role; then change roles.

6. Divide the class in half and have them take the two roles; then have them switch roles.

7. Have volunteers say the dialogue for the class.

8. Have class open books and practice the dialogue in pairs.

*Cassette users can have the students listen to the dialogue first with books closed.

☛ **Practice: "It's a 29–cent stamp"**

1. Explain the difference between cent used as an adjective (*a 32–cent stamp*) and cent used as a plural noun (It's *50 cents*).

2. Have students practice the conversations in the text.

Something New: Packages

Page 35

1. Use visuals V42–V44 to explain differences among the three types of packages.

2. Show visuals and say "Parcel Post," "Express Mail," and "Priority Mail," and have students repeat.

3. Follow the procedure for Something New: Postal Services above.

4. Talk about which way is the cheapest, most expensive, fastest, slowest method of sending a package, using Discussion questions #1–3 as a guide.

Page 36
★ Something Extra: How to Send a Package

1. Set the scene: Two people are at the post office. Jae is sending a vase to Korea, and Jim is sending a photograph to Mexico.

2. Read the post office directions to the class. Explain new vocabulary.

3. Have students read #1 and then ask "What does Jae do?" "What does Jim do?" Explain new vocabulary as the student reads what each does.

4. Follow the same procedure for #2–5.

Page 37
☛ Practice Activity: Send a package

1. Divide the class into groups of 4–5 students.

2. Have students discuss #1–2.

☛ Practice Activity: Which Service to Use?

Have students match the need on the left to the appropriate service on the right. Do the first one as an example.

📼 Reading: A Money Order*

1. Read the passage to the class as students follow along in their books.

2. Check comprehension by asking oral questions about the passage.

3. Have students read the passage on their own.

*Cassette users can have students listen to the Reading first with books closed, and then listen again and read along silently.

Discussion

Facilitate a discussion of the reading passage and money orders, using questions #1–6 as a guide.

Page 38
Reading: Felix's Letter

Have a volunteer read Felix's letter to his parents. Ask oral comprehension questions.

✍ **Writing:** Write a letter

1. Have students write a short letter to a friend or relative.

2. This can be done for homework.

3. The next day have volunteers read their letters to the class.

Lesson 4 Activity Page

Page 39 **A. Listen and put the correct number under the person talking.***
Read script or play the tape and have students look carefully at the illustration to decide who's speaking in each case.

Script:
1. I'm mailing some postcards to my friends. They're valentines. I think they're less expensive than letters, and I have so many friends.

2. I wish this line would move! I'm a busy man. I'm in a hurry and I need to mail these papers right away. I'll use Express Mail and the papers will be in New York tomorrow!

3. I need aerograms. I always write to my family and friends in Venezuela. I have $15.00, so I can buy 10 aerograms and some stamps today.

4. I'm standing in the front of the line, but it isn't moving. Why is there only one window open? This box is heavy, but my mother will be surprised when she sees her present. Good thing her birthday isn't for another week; I can use Parcel Post.

5. I'm at the end of the line, and I sure hope the line moves soon. I'm late for my baseball game. I need to buy stamps for these letters. My mom asked me to get her the stamps and mail the letters, but I didn't know about the lines in this place. Sheesh!

*Cassette users can have students listen to the script on tape.

B. Look at the picture and write the correct words in the story below.

1. Explain that students need to refer to the picture above.

2. Students will choose from the words in the box to fill in the blanks. Do the first sentence as an example.

Lesson 5

I'm Homesick

Communication Objectives:
    Talk about how you feel
    Make suggestions
    Interpret a mail collection schedule

New Structures:
    Why don't you...?

Visuals:

V45	I'm sick.
V46	Go to the doctor.
V47	I'm tired and sleepy.
V48	Go to bed early.
V49	I'm thirsty.
V50	Drink some water.
V51	I'm hungry.
V52	Eat something.
V53	I'm cold.
V54	Put on this sweater.
V55	I'm warm.
V56	Turn on the fan.
V57	Let's Talk: I Want To Get a Letter from Home

Other instructional aids: Examples of junk mail, masking tape (to put visuals on the chalkboard)

Page 40

✔ Review: Postal Services

1. Write services on the chalkboard and discuss.

2. Review steps in preparing a package for mailing.

3. Discuss sending money by mail.

Something New: What's the Matter?

1. Explain lesson objective: To discuss feelings and make suggestions.

2. Ask "What's the matter?" Hold up V45 and say "I'm sick." Have students repeat.

3. Hold up V46 and say "Go to the doctor." Have students repeat.

4. Hold up V45 and V46 together and say "I'm sick." "Go to the doctor."*

5. Repeat the process with V47, V49, V51, V53, V55 (problems), and V48, V50, V52, V54, V56 (suggestions).

6. Repeat the problems and have students give the suggestions.

*You can tape two visuals to chalkboard and show a face under the problem visual, and another face under the suggestion visual (to indicate a second speaker). Then point to each as you say the problem or suggestion.

Optional: Have volunteers come up to the front and choose a problem visual from a face–down pile on the desk. The student then has to find the matching suggestion visual and tape them both on the chalkboard side by side.

Let's Talk: I Want to Get a Letter from Home*

Page 42

1. Show the visual to establish the context of the conversation: May is home-sick (explain) and wants to get a letter from home.

2. Model the dialogue as students listen, indicating the speakers by pointing to the visual or other means.

3. Model the dialogue again.

4. Model the dialogue and have class repeat.

5. Take one role and have class take the other role; then change roles.

6. Divide the class in half and have them take the two roles; then have them switch roles.

7. Have volunteers say the dialogue for the class.

8. Have class open books and practice the dialogue in pairs.

*Cassette users can have the students listen to the dialogue first with books closed.

☛ Practice: "She wants to get a letter"

1. Explain that *What's the matter?* is the same as *Is anything the matter?*

2. Have students practice the conversations in pairs. They can interchange the *Why don't you...?* suggestion with the imperative (the first being a little softer.)

Page 43

Interaction: Making Suggestions

 Have students walk around the room and do the activity as stated in the text.

Reading: Send Mail*

1. Read the passage to the class as students follow along in their books.

2. Check comprehension by asking oral questions about the passage.

3. Have students read the passage on their own.

*Cassette users can have students listen to the Reading first with books closed, and then listen again and read along silently.

Page 44

Discussion

1. Have volunteers answer the questions orally.

2. For #7, ask a few students their opinions.

☛ Practice Activity: Mail Collection Times

1. Students need to refer to the schedule in the Reading in order to answer the questions.

2. Have volunteers write their answers on the chalkboard.

Page 45

✍ Writing

1. Students will fill in the appropriate question or response to complete the dialogues. Do #1 as an example.

2. For #1 and #2, they need to write one line. For #3 and #4, they need to write the middle lines.

Page 46

★ Something Extra: Junk Mail

1. Explain *junk mail*. Use the pictures in the book as examples, or bring your own.

2. Read the passage to the class. Ask a few oral comprehension questions.

Discussion

1. Have students answer the questions orally.

2. Show your own junk mail, and ask students to bring in some the next day.

Lesson 5 Activity Pages

Page 47 ***A. Listen to the complaints and check the problem.****

1. Students will hear six people talk about their feelings or problems. They will check the appropriate box under the feeling for each person.

2. The first one is an example. Read the script or play the tape.

Script:

1. I really want a turkey sandwich right now. I can't wait for lunch. It's almost 12:00!

2. I need to put on a sweater. Brrrrr. It must be 30 degrees in here. Put on the heater, please.

3. I have a fever. I need to see the doctor. I can't work today. I feel terrible!

4. I need a drink of water. I was out in the sun all day. I like to garden, but boy, do I need to drink something!

5. Wow! It's 100 degrees out here! I don't like the summer weather. I need to go swimming right now!

6. I didn't go to bed last night. (Yawn) I can't work today. I need to go home early and go to bed!

*Cassette users can have students listen to the script on tape.

B. Talk with your partner.

1. Pair students. One looks only at page 47, and the other looks only at page 48. One student needs to ask "What's the matter?," while the other gives the answer. Then both discuss a suggestion of what that person needs to do. Student A asks for Paula and Max, while Student B asks for Gladys and Tina. Harry is done as an example.

2. Go over completed conversations with the class.

Page 48

C. Match the problems and the suggestions.

Do the first one as an example. Then have students write the correct number in each blank.

D. Talk with your partner.

See B.

Delta's Apple Pie, Teacher's Guide 2A

E. Read the letters and write your answers.

This is like a *Dear Abby* column. Students must give their advice.

F. Talk about your suggestions to Thanh, Miguel, and Sara with the class.

Talk about the various responses when students finish.

I Need to Get Some Medicine

Communication Objectives:
Give/follow directions
Identify sections of a drugstore
Identify items sold in a drugstore

New Structures:
Prepositional phrases *in the front of the store,* etc.

Visuals:
V58   Something New: A Drugstore
V59   Let's Talk: Go to the Pharmacy Section

Other instructional aids: Examples of housewares, prescription medicines, over–the–counter medicines, cosmetics, liquor, stationery, or pictures of same.

Page 50

✔ Review

How Do You Feel?
Have pairs ask each other how they feel and make suggestions to help.

Junk Mail
Have students share their junk mail samples with 2–3 others. Discuss the questions in the text.

Page 51

Something New: A Drugstore

1. Briefly explain the lesson objective: To identify sections of a drugstore and give and follow directions.

2. Show V58, or use a transparency of it. Name the sections as students listen.

3. Review the sections one at a time and have students repeat.

4. Explain the vocabulary of each section, and have students repeat.

5. Ask comprehension questions.

☛ Practice Activity: Giving Directions

1. Have one student read the "I need to get…" part on the left, and have another student give the correct response "Go to the…" on the right. The first one is an example.

2. Give some other examples that are not suggested in the text.

Page 52 **Let's Talk:** Go to the Pharmacy Section*

1. Show the visual to establish the context of the conversation: Mrs. To is in the drugstore. She needs some medicine and is asking the clerk where she can find some.

2. Model the dialogue as students listen, indicating the speakers by pointing to the visual or other means.

3. Model the dialogue again.

4. Model the dialogue and have class repeat.

5. Take one role and have class take the other role; then change roles.

6. Divide the class in half and have them take the two roles; then have them switch roles.

7. Have volunteers say the dialogue for the class.

8. Have class open books and practice the dialogue in pairs.

*Cassette users can have the students listen to the dialogue first with books closed.

☛ Practice: "Go to the cosmetics section"

1. Review right, left, center, back, front, corner, and other locations you may need.

2. Have students practice the dialogues in pairs, switching roles back and forth.

Page 53 ## ☛ Practice Activity: A Shopping List

1. Divide class into groups of 4–5 students each.

2. Have each group do the activity.

3. Have groups report back to share their answers with the class.

4. Make a list on the chalkboard and write some directions.

📼 Reading: American Drugstores*

1. Explain new vocabulary.

2. Read the passage to the class as students follow along in their books.

3. Check comprehension by asking oral questions about the passage.

4. Have students read the passage on their own.

*Cassette users can have students listen to the Reading first with books closed, and then listen again and read along silently.

Discussion

1. Facilitate a discussion of American drugstores using questions #1–5 as a guide.

2. For #6, students answer for their native country.

Page 54

✍ Writing

1. Have students write the appropriate question or answer for #1–4.

2. Then have students write the need on the left, or the instruction on the right.

3. Correct on chalkboard or overhead.

Lesson 6 Activity Pages

Page 55 📼 *A. Look at the key. Listen and mark the correct locations.*

1. Explain that students will hear information about the location of drugstore items. They need to put the correct numbers on the key as they listen to the script.

2. Read script or play the tape. Then correct together.

Script:
1. This is the ABC Drugstore in my neighborhood. I go here once or twice a week. The stationery section is my favorite place in the store. I love the funny cards. The stationery section is in the center of the store, on the right.

2. When I need some lipstick (I like to try new colors), I go to the cosmetics section. It's next to the stationery, in the back corner.

3. Sometimes I need to pick up some paper towels or cleaning supplies, and I just walk over to the household goods. They're in the center of the store on the left.

4. Sometimes we run out of aspirin, and so I go to the cold medicine, on the back wall, in the left corner. I get a headache just looking at the price of aspirin these days!

5. The only time I don't like to go to the drugstore is when I need to get prescription medicine. Our pharmacy is on the back wall, in the center. There's always a long line, and you know, when you're sick, you don't want to wait.

6. Sometimes my family and I go to the drugstore just to get an ice cream cone! They sell delicious ice cream at ABC. The ice cream counter is in the front of the store, on the left. Sure, my family goes to ABC Drugstore for prescriptions and cold medicine, but sometimes, ice cream is the best medicine!

7. When we take pictures at home, I always take them to the drugstore for developing. The photo section has good prices on film, batteries, and cameras, too. It's in the center of the store.

*Cassette users can have students listen to the the script on tape.

B. Look at the picture. Write the answers.
Students will write the answers based on the locations in Exercise A.

C. Write the items under the correct sections.
Students will place the items in the box under the correct section above.

Page 56

Unit Two  Evaluation

Page 57 **I. Listening Comprehension***

    1. Students will circle A or B for #1–7, and the correct response for #8.

    2. Read the script or play the tape.

        Script:

        1. I don't want to pay very much.

        2. I want to send a birthday card to Peru.

        3. It's a fast way to send mail.

        4. I'm sick.

        5. It's Airmail to Mexico.

        6. I need to get some shampoo.

        7. She has a prescription. Where does she go?

        8. Is there a Sunday morning pick–up?

    *Cassette users can have students listen to the script on the tape.

Page 58 **II. Reading and III. Writing**

    1. Go over the directions for Part II and III with students.

    2. Have class do these sections independently.

Evaluation Check

    1. Correct evaluation by having student volunteers write their answers on the board or an overhead transparency.

    2. Have class check their answers.

    3. Circulate to make sure students have checked their work accurately.

I Need to Go to San Francisco

Communication objectives:
>   Make airline reservations
>   Use an airport map

New Structures:
>   None

Visuals:
V60	a round–trip reservation for Mexico City
V61	a one–way reservation for Seattle
V62	the smoking section
V63	the non–smoking section
V64	an aisle seat
V65	a window seat
V66	Let's Talk: At the Ticket Counter

Page 60

✔ Review: Where Are You Going?

1. Students will review community places, what you need to get at each place, and what you want to do.

2. Have students look at the illustration of the hardware store and say "I'm going to the hardware store." "I need to get some nails." "I want to put up a painting." Have students repeat.

3. Follow the same procedure with post office and bank.

4. Optional: Elicit other places from students and list them on the chalkboard, along with the second and third parts of the exercise.

5. Have students practice in pairs, adding additional examples if they can.

Page 61

Something New: Airline Reservations

1. Briefly explain the lesson objective: To make an airline reservation. Explain reservation.

2. Have students listen as you hold up V60 and say "A round–trip reservation for Mexico City."

3. Show V60 and have students repeat "A round–trip reservation for Mexico City."

4. Show V61 and say "A one–way reservation for Seattle." Show it again and have students repeat. Explain the difference between round–trip and one–way.

5. Follow the same procedure with V62, V63, V64, V65, explaining the differences between each pair.

Page 62

☛ Practice Activity: Substitutions

1. Write the complete sentence for #1 on the chalkboard and say it.

2. Have students repeat.

3. This is a multiple–slot substitution exercise. Each time you repeat the sentence, you will change one item in the sentence and students will repeat the whole sentence with the change. As they get used to the pattern, you will say only the cue word, and students will give the entire sentence.

4. Do #1 as an example; then practice with the whole class.

📼 Let's Talk: At the Ticket Counter*

1. Show the visual to establish the context of the conversation: Anita is making an airline reservation at the Pacific Airlines office.

2. Model the dialogue as students listen, indicating the speakers by pointing to the visual or other means.

3. Model the dialogue again.

4. Model the dialogue and have class repeat.

5. Take one role and have class take the other role; then change roles.

6. Divide the class in half and have them take the two roles; then have them switch roles.

7. Have volunteers say the dialogue for the class.

8. Have class open books and practice the dialogue in pairs.

*Cassette users can have the students listen to the dialogue first with books closed.

☛ Practice: "When do you need to leave?"

1. Review ordinal numbers for dates.

2. Have students practice the dialogues in pairs. They can change any of the information they want, to get varied practices.

☛ Practice Activity: Making Reservations

Have pairs of students use the questions in the text to ask and answer questions about making airline reservations.

Reading: At the Airport

1. Show the visual from the text on a transparency, or hold it up. Identify all the areas and explain.

2. Ask oral comprehension questions.

Discussion

1. Read the introduction line.

2. Read the questions and have students answer orally.

✍ Writing

1. Students will fill in the blanks using the airline diagram as a guide.

2. Correct together.

✍✍ More Writing

1. Students will use the visuals given to fill in the blanks for each question.

2. Correct together.

Page 67 ***A. Listen and circle the correct information.****

    1. Students need to complete the date of departure and date of return, and circle M, A, or E for morning, afternoon, or evening flights. You may wish to do the exercise twice and have students listen for dates only the first time and for the time of day the second time.

    2. Read the script, or play the tape. Read the whole script as necessary.

Script:

    1. I'm planning to fly to Seattle on December 26th in the morning, and I'll fly back home to L.A. on January 3rd, in the evening.

    2. I want to go to San Francisco on May 13th in the afternoon, and return to San Diego on May 14th in the morning.

    3. I'd like to make a reservation for a round–trip flight to Los Angeles on October 10th, in the evening, returning to New York on October 21st, in the afternoon.

    4. I need to go to New York for a few days on business. I'm leaving at 6:00 a.m. on July 21st, and I'm coming back at 11:00 a.m. on July 25th.

    5. I'm going on a trip to London! Our plane leaves at 3:00 p.m. on November 25th and our return flight is at 5:00 p.m. on December 25th. A whole month in London!

    6. My husband and I are going to Paris for our anniversary. We have reservations on the 7:30 p.m. flight to Paris on April 3rd and we're staying until April 14th, at 9:30 p.m.

    *Cassette users can have students listen to the script on tape.

B. Put the sentences in the correct order.

    Students will order the steps of taking a flight from #1–9.

Page 68   ***C. Ask and answer the questions with your partner.***

    1. Have students work in pairs to do the exercise.

    2. Have a few pairs share their answers with the class.

Lesson 8

The Flight Leaves at 8:45

Communication Objectives:
Read a flight schedule
Read a travel itinerary

New Structures:
Simple present used as future

Visuals:
V67   Something New: Reading an Airline Schedule
V68   Let's Talk: Flight 48

Page 70   ✔ **Review:** A Dream Vacation

Have students do the roleplay in pairs.

Something New: Reading an Airline Schedule

1. Briefly explain the lesson objective: To read and understand an airline schedule.

2. Hold up the visual or show a transparency of it.

3. Explain the five headings. Have students repeat the headings.

4. Flight 56 information is given as an example. Do another one.

5. Ask oral comprehension questions (yes/no and "wh" type).

6. Ask the comprehension questions on page 71.

Page 71   ☛ **Practice: "What time does it leave?"**

Have students practice the questions using the five flights given in the visual. If necessary, review the structure of the questions using #1–4 above.

🔲 **Let's Talk:** Flight 48*

1. Show the visual to establish the context of the conversation: Anita, in Los Angeles, is talking on the phone to her friend Jane, in San Francisco. Anita is going to visit Jane in San Francisco.

2. Model the dialogue as students listen, indicating the speakers by pointing to the visual or other means.

3. Model the dialogue again.

4. Model the dialogue and have class repeat.

5. Take one role and have class take the other role; then change roles.

6. Divide the class in half and have them take the two roles; then have them switch roles.

7. Have volunteers say the dialogue for the class.

8. Have class open books and practice the dialogue in pairs.

*Cassette users can have the students listen to the dialogue first with books closed.

Page 72 ☛ **Practice: "Where does flight 278 go?"**

1. Have students practice the conversations in pairs. #1–4 are from the visual; #5–6 are new.

2. Check pronunciation of *leaves* and *arrives*.

☛ **Practice Activity: A Travel Itinerary**

1. Explain *itinerary* and *travel agency*.

2. Show the visual from the text or on a transparency. Discuss the information on the itinerary and ask oral comprehension questions using the discussion questions on page 73 as a guide. Have pairs ask and answer questions if you wish.

Page 73 🔲 **Reading:** Traveling*

1. Read the passage to the class as students follow along in their books.

2. Check comprehension by asking oral questions about the passage. Ask the discussion questions for students to answer orally.

3. Have students read the passage on their own.

*Cassette users can have students listen to the Reading first with books closed, and then listen again and read along silently.

36

Delta's Apple Pie, Teacher's Guide 2A

✍ Writing

Have students answer the questions from the Reading. In #5 students must complete the question and the short answer.

Lesson 8 Activity Pages

Page 74 ***A. Listen to the airport announcement. Circle the correct information.****
Go over the instructions, and then read the script or play the tape.

Script:

1. Announcing American Airlines Flight 17 arriving at Gate 54. (repeat)

2. Announcing a change in gates for US Air Flight 65. US Air Flight 65 will now arrive at Gate 13. (repeat)

3. TWA Flight 70 is now ready for boarding at Gate 2. Passengers holding tickets for aisles 17–37 may now board. (repeat)

4. Last call for Flight 414. All passengers holding tickets for Flight 414 should now board at Gate 40. (repeat)

5. We have an announcement for passengers holding tickets on Flight 307 flying into Phoenix. Your flight is delayed and will be departing at 10:30 P.M. (repeat)

6. All passengers, the white zone is for loading and unloading of passengers only. Cars staying longer than five minutes in the loading zone will be ticketed.

*Cassette users can have students listen to the script on tape.

B. Talk with your partner.

1. Pair students. One looks at B on page 74 and the other looks at E on page 75. They take turns asking and answering questions about the missing information. Flight 98 is an example.

2. Correct together.

C. Look at the completed flight schedule and answer the questions.

Students will answer the questions from the completed schedule in exercise B above or E on page 75.

D. Match the questions to the answers.

Students will match the questions on the left to the appropriate answer on the right.

E. Talk with your partner.

See B.

F. Look at the completed flight departure schedule and write questions.

Students will write the questions from the completed schedule above.

Lesson 9

What Do You Have to Do?

Communication Objective:
Discuss necessary tasks

New Structures:
Have to for present and future
Questions with *have to*
It takes + length of time
Preposition *by* with time

Visuals:

V69   Sara has to pick up the tickets.
V70   Tomas has to buy swimming trunks.
V71   Sara has to buy a bathing suit.
V72   Sara and Tomas have to pack.
V73   Let's Talk: Can You Take Us to the Airport?

Page 76

✔ Review: A Plane Trip

Have students work in pairs to do the Review exercise.

Something New: Things to Do

1. Briefly explain the lesson objective: To talk about things you have to do before a trip.

2. Read the short passage about Sara and Tomas. Show V69 and say, "Two weeks before the the trip, Sara has to pick up the tickets."

3. Show V69 again and repeat "She has to pick up the tickets." Have students repeat.

4. Repeat the process with V70 and V71.

5. Ask "What does Sara have to do?" Show the visuals with Sara. Elicit correct response. Repeat with Tomas visual.

6. Show V72 and say, "The day before the trip, Sara and Tomas have to pack."

7. Show V72 again and repeat "They have to pack." Have students repeat.

8. Review all four visuals.

 Page 77 📼 **Let's Talk:** Can You Take Us to the Airport?*

1. Show the visual to establish the context of the conversation: Tomas is talking to his friend Tony. He is asking Tony to take Sara and him to the airport.

2. Model the dialogue as students listen, indicating the speakers by pointing to the visual or other means.

3. Model the dialogue again.

4. Model the dialogue and have class repeat.

5. Take one role and have class take the other role; then change roles.

6. Divide the class in half and have them take the two roles; then have them switch roles.

7. Have volunteers say the dialogue for the class.

 8. Have class open books and practice the dialogue in pairs.

*Cassette users can have the students listen to the dialogue first with books closed.

Page 78 ☛ **Practice: "When do you have to check in?**

1. Explain *check in* for a flight.

2. Have students practice the conversations in pairs.

Page 79 ☛ **Practice: "What do you have to do today?"**

1. Explain use of *have to* for present or future time.

2. Have students practice the conversations in pairs.

☛ **Practice Activity: Things to Do Today**

1. Divide class into groups of 4–5 students each.

 2. Have each member list what he/she has to do today; then share within the group.

3. List some of the ideas on the chalkboard.

✍ Writing

Have students write sentences about five people. Be sure they practice *he/she has to* instead of *I have to*, as in the previous exercise.

★ Something Extra: Planning a Party

1. Divide class into groups of 4–5 students each (may be same groups as for previous activity if done the same day).

 2. Explain that they will be planning a party and will assign each group member a task to do.

3. Afterward, have volunteers share their ideas.

📼 Reading: Getting Ready for a Vacation*

1. Read the passage to the class as students follow along in their books. Explain new vocabulary.

2. Check comprehension by asking oral questions about the passage.

3. Have students read the passage on their own.

*Cassette users can have students listen to the Reading first with books closed, and then listen again and read along silently.

✍ Writing

1. Have students complete questions and answers #1–4.

2. Go over the directions given for #5 and have students fill out the list on page 82 for Mr. and Mrs. Johnson's pre–trip tasks. Encourage them to add as many things to the list as they can think of.

Lesson 9 Activity Pages

A. Match the sentences.
Martha is complaining to her mom. Her mom is giving her advice. Students will match the problem on the left to the advice on the right. #1 is an example.

B. Ask and answer the questions with your classmates.
 1. Explain directions to the class. They will need to walk around to talk to a lot of different classmates in order to fill out the chart.

2. Explain any items students might not understand.

3. Give small prizes for winners.

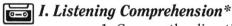

Page 85 **I. Listening Comprehension***

1. Go over the directions for Part I with students.

2. Read each item of the script two times, at normal conversational speed.

Script:

1. I need to make a round–trip reservation.

2. I'd like an aisle seat.

3. It goes to Denver.

4. What time does it leave?

5. He's taking Flight 410. Where does he need to go?

6. It arrives in Miami at 6:45 p.m.

7. He has to pack for his trip.

8. I have to wash the car today.

*Cassette users can have students listen to the script on the tape.

Page 86 **II. Reading and III. Writing**

1. Go over the directions for Parts II and III with students.

2. Have class do these sections independently.

Evaluation Check

1. Correct evaluation by having student volunteers write their answers on the board or an overhead transparency.

2. Have class check their answers.

3. Circulate to make sure students have checked their work accurately.

Lesson 10

What Did He Do Last Night?

Communication Objectives:
>Talk about past activities to socialize
>Ask about weekend activities

New Structures:
>Simple past (regular verbs)
>Questions with *did*

Visuals:

V74	Peter washed his car.
V75	Olga studied.
V76	Then they played cards.
V77	Ben cleaned the yard.
V78	Sue vacuumed.
V79	Then they visited friends.
V80	They washed the dishes.
V81	He watched TV.
V82	She sewed.
V83	Let's Talk: Did You Practice English Last Night?

Page 88

✔ Review: What I Do Every Day

Have students do the review in groups of three.

Something New: What Was the Date Last Friday?

1. Briefly explain the lesson objective: To talk about activities in the past.

2. Put the mini–calendar on the chalkboard, or show a transparency.

3. Write the date for Sunday, last week and this week. Contrast the two.

4. Have students open the book and do the same with a partner.

Page 89

Something New: What Did You Do Last Week?

1. Hold up V74 and say "Last Friday, Peter washed his car." Repeat "He washed his car."

2. Ask "What did he do?" Answer and have students repeat.

3. Follow this pattern with the other visuals. Use the correct pronouns for each visual.

4. Review all visuals and elicit correct responses.

 5. Have students open books and read what they have been practicing orally. Point out the spelling of the past form.

Page 90 ☛ **Practice: "Did she wash the dishes?"**

Have students practice the conversations in pairs.

 Let's Talk: Did You Practice English Last Night?*

1. Show the visual to establish the context of the conversation: Two students are talking before class begins.

2. Model the dialogue as students listen, indicating the speakers by pointing to the visual or other means.

3. Model the dialogue again.

4. Model the dialogue and have class repeat.

5. Take one role and have class take the other role; then change roles.

6. Divide the class in half and have them take the two roles; then have them switch roles.

7. Have volunteers say the dialogue for the class.

 8. Have class open books and practice the dialogue in pairs.

*Cassette users can have students listen to the dialogue first with books closed.

Page 91 ☛ **Practice Activity: Substitutions**

1. This is a multiple–slot substitution drill. Write #1 on the chalkboard and do it as an example, changing one item each time you repeat the sentence. Do it again with the class.

2. Do #2 and #3 in the same manner.

☛ **Practice Activity: What did they do in the evening?**

1. Go over all the pictures in the activity.

2. Have volunteers read the three questions for the Garcias and answer in the past tense.

3. Follow the same procedure with Henry and Bill. Note the difference between present and past tense for Bill.

Page 92

■ Interaction: What Did You Do Last Weekend?

1. Students will walk around the room, asking four classmates about their past weekends.

2. Be sure that students ask questions beginning with *Did you...?* They also need to ask *When did you...?*

3. Do one on the chalkboard as an example. Practice the questins orally before students begin.

Page 93

Reading: The Martin Family's Weekend*

1. Read the passage to the class as students follow along in their books. Explain new vocabulary.

2. Check comprehension by asking oral questions about the passage.

3. Have students read the passage on their own.

*Cassette users can have students listen to the Reading first with books closed, and then listen again and read along silently.

✍ Writing

Have students write the correct answers or questions for each item.

Lesson 10 Activity Pages

Page 94 **A. Listen to Charlie's day and number the pictures.***

> 1. Students will listen to each item and put the numbers 1–8 under the picture described.

> 2. Read the script or play the tape.

> > **Script:**
> > 1. Last Sunday was very nice! I cleaned the yard in the afternoon.
> >
> > 2. I was tired when I finished, so I rested in the living room and watched TV.
> >
> > 3. I studied English for an hour before dinner. I practiced reading and writing.
> >
> > 4. At 6:00 I cooked a delicious dinner…salad, chicken and rice. Mmmmm.
> >
> > 5. I started to eat when…(telephone ring) naturally, the phone started to ring.
> >
> > 6. I answered the phone and talked to my friend Michelle. She invited me to her house.
> >
> > 7. I walked to her house about 7:30. She lives nearby, so I like to walk to her house.
> >
> > 8. I visited my friend for an hour and then we played cards.

> *Cassette users can have students listen to the script on tape.

Page 95 **B. Write the missing words in Charlie's story.**
> Students will choose from the verbs above to write in the blanks in the story.

Lesson 11

What School Did He Attend?

Communication Objectives:
Talk about U.S. school system
Talk about own educational history
Pronounce *–ed* on verbs

New Structures:
Adverbs *still* and *anymore*

Visuals:

V84	Chapman Street Elementary School
V85	Chapman Street Elementary School
V86	Oakwood Middle School
V87	Washington High School
V88	Let's Talk: He Graduated in June

Page 96

✔ Review: Last Week

Students will walk around and talk to three classmates, asking questions about things they did last week. Give examples of both *yes/no* and *What...* questions.

Something New: U.S. Schools

1. Briefly explain lesson objective: To discuss the U.S. school system, and talk about schools people attend and attended.

2. Show V84. Say "Henry is 5 years old. He's in kindergarten. He attends elementary school."

3. Show the visual again. Repeat "He attends elementary school." Have students repeat.

4. Show V85 and say "Bill is 10 years old. He's in 5th grade. He attends elementary school."

5. Show the visual again. Repeat "He attends elementary school." Have students repeat.

6. Follow the same pattern with V86 and V87.

7. Review all four visuals, all four students, and elicit correct responses.

Page 97 **Let's Talk:** He Graduated in June*

1. Show the visual to establish the context of the conversation: Bill and Ken are talking about Ken's son Peter.

2. Model the dialogue as students listen, indicating the speakers by pointing to the visual or other means.

3. Explain *graduate, scholarship,* and *tuition.* Have students guess their meanings from the context, if possible.

4. Model the dialogue again.

5. Model the dialogue and have class repeat.

6. Take one role and have class take the other role; then change roles.

7. Divide the class in half and have them take the two roles; then have them switch roles.

8. Have volunteers say the dialogue for the class.

 9. Have class open books and practice the dialogue in pairs.

*Cassette users can have the students listen to the dialogue first with books closed.

Page 98 ☛ **Practice: "What grade is he in?"**

1. Point out that we usually use ordinal numbers for grade level.

2. Have students practice the conversations in pairs.

☛ **Practice Activity: Talking about School**

Have pairs of students ask and answer questions about their own schooling.

Page 99 ★ **Something Extra:** Pronunciation of the Past Tense

1. Read examples to the class, emphasizing the three pronunciation variations.

2. Do the three examples below with the class.

3. Do a "dictation" for the listening practice. Students will listen to the eight verbs and will choose which variant they hear and will mark 1, 2, or 3 on their paper.

1. cleaned	5. visited
2. washed	6. rested
3. played	7. cooked
4. studied	8. finished

☛ Practice Activity: Actions

1. Students will give instructions to their partner, and the partner will tell what he/she did.

2. Do the example for the class and have students do the rest.

3. Students will now write sentences in the past about what they did.

Page 100 🎞 **Reading:** Schools in the United States*

1. Read the passage to the class as students follow along in their books.

2. Check comprehension by asking oral questions about the passage.

3. Have students read the passage on their own.

*Cassette users can have students listen to the Reading first with books closed, and then listen again and read along silently.

Discussion

1. #1–3 are based on the Reading.

2. #4–5 are for students' native countries.

✍ Writing

1. This can be done for homework.

2. Students will write about schools they attended.

3. The next day, have volunteers read their stories.

Lesson 11 Activity Pages

Page 101 🔲 **A. Read and listen to the verbs. Make a check under the sound you hear.***

Read the script or play the tape. Have the students listen to the ending of each past form and mark which pronunciation they hear, "d," "t," or "ɪd." Be sure to read at normal speed and not to exaggerate the pronunciation of the –*ed* ending. If students have trouble, read the entire script again.

Script:

1. He played basketball.

2. He needed to sit down.

3. He watched the game.

4. He cleaned his house.

5. He showed me his house.

6. He missed the bus.

7. He walked to the store.

8. He shopped for a present.

9. He called a taxi.

10. He visited his friends.

11. His watch stopped.

12. He looked at a clock.

*Cassette users can have students listen to the script on tape.

B. Talk about the chart with your partner.

1. Pairs of students will discuss the information about Martin, Feliz, and Liseth. They will ask *yes/no* questions about their education.

2. Do one or two questions and answers as an example.

Page 102 **C. Answer the questions and then compare your answers to your partner's.**

Students are still in pairs. They will answer the questions for themselves, and then compare their answers to their partner's.

D. Ask and answer the questions with your classmates.

    1. Explain the TIC TAC TOE game. Students must ask *yes/no* questions and only write the names of those who answer *yes*.

    2. Give small prizes to winners.

Page 103   **E. Use the names and the information to write about the people in class.**

    1. Students will write a complete sentence using the answers from the TIC TAC TOE game.

    2. Optional: Introduce *Nobody/No one*, as in "Nobody played cards."

Lesson 12

Learning Never Ends

Communication Objectives:
> Discuss adult education in the U.S.
> Ask about vocational training
> Discuss future plans

New Structures:
> *Want to be* + occupation

Visuals:

V89	She studied nursing at a community college.
V90	I studied welding at an occupational center.
V91	He studied television repair at an vocational school.
V92	They studied English at an adult school.
V93	Let's Talk: Did You Complete the Course?
V94	Let's Talk: I Want to Be…

Other instructional aids: Pictures of occupations from **Apple Pie 1A** or other sources

Page 104   ✔ **Review**

Neighborhood Children
Have students do #1 based on the pictures in the text.

What did you do last night?
Have students ask four classmates what they did last night. They will fill in the grid. Do an example for the class.

Page 105   ## Something New: Job Plans

1. Briefly explain the lesson objective: To discuss schools for adults.

2. Show V89, V90, V91, and V92 and explain the three kinds of schools for adults covered in the visuals. Explain the differences among them.

3. Show V89 and say "She studied nursing at a community college." Ask "What did she study?" Give answer. Ask "Where did she study?" Give answer. Have students repeat.

4. Follow the same procedure with V90, V91, and V92.

5. Review the four visuals and ask the *what* and *where* questions again.

Page 106 **Let's Talk:** Did You Complete the Course?*

1. Show the visual to establish the context of the conversation: Lenore studied vocational nursing and is now talking to an employment counselor about a job.

2. Model the dialogue as students listen, indicating the speakers by pointing to the visual or other means.

3. Explain any new vocabulary items. Elicit their meanings from the context, if possible.

4. Model the dialogue again.

5. Model the dialogue and have class repeat.

6. Take one role and have class take the other role; then change roles.

7. Divide the class in half and have them take the two roles; then have them switch roles.

8. Have volunteers say the dialogue for the class.

 9. Have class open books and practice the dialogue in pairs.

*Cassette users can have the students listen to the dialogue first with books closed.

Discussion

Have volunteers answer the questions orally.

☛ Practice: "Did he receive his license?"

Have students practice the dialogues in pairs.

Page 107 ### ★ Something Extra: Planning for the Future

1. Read the sentences as students follow along in their books.

2. Explain new occupations and have students repeat.

3. Point to the pictures and ask "What do/does you/he/she want to be?" Elicit correct responses.

4. Show more visuals of different occupations and ask "What does he/she want to be?" Elicit correct responses.

Page 108

Let's Talk: I Want to Be...

1. Show the visual to establish the context of the conversation. Ted is talking to the adult school counselor about his future plans.

2. Follow the same procedure as in the previous Let's Talk: Did You Complete the Course?

☞ Practice Activity: Career Plans

Have students do the activity in pairs. Have volunteers share their responses with the class. Write some on the chalkboard.

📼 Reading: It's Never Too Late*

1. Read the passage to the class as students follow along in their books.

2. Check comprehension by asking oral questions about the passage.

3. Have students read the passage on their own.

*Cassette users can have students listen to the Reading first with books closed, and then listen again and read along silently.

Discussion

Facilitate a discussion of adult schools using the questions as a guide.

Page 109

✐ Writing

1. Have students fill in the missing question or answer for each item.

2. Have students write the missing word in the cloze passage.

Lesson 12 Activity Pages

Page 110

A. Fill out the form with your education and experience.
Go over the questions on the form and then have students fill it out with their own educational histories and work experience.

Page 111

B. Make questions from the statements.

1. Students will write the past tense question for each statement and then will walk around to ask classmates these questions. They will write the names of students who answer "yes" to the questions.

2. Go over as a class.

Unit Four **Evaluation**

Page 113 🔲 **I. Listening Comprehension***

1. Go over the directions for Part I with students.

2. Read each item of the script two times, at normal conversational speed.

Script:
1. He cleaned the yard on Saturday.

2. She vacuumed the house on Saturday.

3. He visited some friends last night.

4. She graduated from high school last year.

5. He worked hard on Sunday.

6. Did Ellen watch TV last night?

7. He passed the state examination.

8. She graduated from nursing school.

*Cassette users can have students listen to the script on the tape.

Page 114 **II. Reading and III. Writing**

1. Go over the directions for Part II and III with students.

2. Have class do these sections independently.

Evaluation Check

1. Correct evaluation by having student volunteers write their answers on the board or an overhead transparency.

2. Have class check their answers.

3. Circulate to make sure students have checked their work accurately.

Lesson 13

What Did You Do Last Sunday?

Communication Objectives:

Talk about recreational activities

Share information about recreational opportunities

New Structures:

Simple past (irregular verbs)

Negatives with *didn't*

Visuals:

V95   We went to the park yesterday.

V96   The children went to the zoo on Sunday.

V97   They went to the carnival last night.

V98   I went to the museum last week.

V99   She went to the swap meet on Saturday.

V100   We went to the movies last month.

V101   Let's Talk: We Went to the Ball Park

Page 116   ✔ **Review:** Every Week; Last Week

Have volunteers answer the questions. Be sure they differentiate between present and past tense. Write their examples on the chalkboard.

Something New: Places to Go for Fun

1. Hold up V95 and say "We went to the park yesterday."

2. Ask "Where did you go yesterday?" Answer "We went to the park." Have students repeat "We went to the park."

3. Follow the same procedure for V96, V97, V98, V99, V100. (Use appropriate pronouns.)

4. Review all six visuals.

Page 117   ☞ **Practice: "Where did you go?"**

Have students practice the conversations in pairs. They can substitute other places, too.

Let's Talk: We Went to the Ball Park *

1. Show the visual to establish the context of the conversation: Ricardo and Don are talking at work on Monday.

2. Model the dialogue as students listen, indicating the speakers by pointing or other means.

3. Model the dialogue again.

4. Model the dialogue and have class repeat.

5. Take one role and have class take the other role; then change roles.

6. Divide the class in half and have them take the two roles; then have them switch roles.

7. Have volunteers say the dialogue for the class.

 8. Have class open books and practice the dialogue in pairs.

*Cassette users can have the students listen to the dialogue first with books closed.

Page 118 ☛ **Practice: "Did Ann and Mark go with you?"**

Have students practice the conversations in pairs.

Something New: What Did You See?

1. Use V96 and V98–V100 again and ask "What did you see at the zoo?" Answer "We saw elephants at the zoo."

2. Have students repeat "We saw elephants."

3. Ask "What did you see at the museum?" Answer "We saw dinosaurs at the museum."

4. Have students repeat "We saw dinosaurs."

5. Follow the same procedure with "movies" and "swap meet."

Page 119 ☛ **Practice: "We saw dinosaurs"**

1. Contrast questions using *Where…go* with *What…see* in the past.

2. Have students practice the conversations in pairs.

★ **Something Extra:** More Weekend Activities

1. Ask again "Where did you go and what did you see?"

2. Show the illustrations in the text, or on a transparency, and read the sentences.

3. Have students repeat.

4. Optional: Say the second part of the sentence and have students supply the first part. Do the same for the other illustrations in the lesson.
   Example:
   T: He saw a lot of fish.
   SS: He went to the aquarium.

Page 120

☞ **Practice: "Where did you go?"**

Have students practice asking and answering questions about where they went and what they did there.

☞ **Practice: "What did you see?"**

Have students practice the conversations in pairs. Note the negative answers.

☞ **Practice Activity: Where did you go?**

1. Divide the class into groups of four.

2. Have members ask each other questions with *where/when/what* in the past.

3. Tony is an example: "Where did you go?" "When did you go there?" "What did you see there?"

4. Have groups share their answers with the class.

Page 121 📼 ## **Reading:** Amusement Parks*

1. Read the passage to the class as students follow along in their books.

2. Check comprehension by asking oral questions about the passage.

3. Have students read the passage on their own.

*Cassette users can have students listen to the Reading first with books closed, and then listen again and read along silently.

Discussion

Facilitate a discussion of amusement parks using the questions as a guide.

✍ Writing

Have students fill in the blanks to complete the conversation.

Page 122 ### ✍✍ More Writing

1. This can be done for homework.

2. The next day have volunteers read their letters to the class.

Lesson 13 Activity Page

Page 123 🔲 **A. *Listen to Rosa talk about where she went last Saturday.*** *
1. Demonstrate how to follow a route.

2. Read the script or play the tape. Repeat the script as necessary, having students circle the things Rosa saw at each place.

> **Script:**
> Listen to Rosa talk about where she went last Saturday. Follow her route with your pencil and circle what she saw.
>
> Wow! Last Saturday was really busy and fun! My cousin and I went all over the city! She is visiting us for a month, but I work all week, so Saturday is our day to play. Last Saturday we went to the bank first. (I needed some money.) I saw my sister–in–law there and we talked for a while.
>
> Next we went to the market to buy our lunch. (We always picnic on Saturdays!) I saw that the bananas were on sale for 25 cents a bunch, and my cousin loves bananas! We picked up a couple of bananas and some other picnic food.
>
> After that we went to the museum. We saw many beautiful paintings. My cousin likes Picasso's paintings, but I like Cezanne's better.
>
> For our next stop we went to the park. We picnicked and saw the children playing on the swings. We love to watch the children play.

My cousin's favorite place is the flea market, so we went there next. She loves jewelry, but she doesn't have a lot of money, so she buys all her jewelry at the flea market. We saw a lot of jewelry that day!

After that we went to the movies. We saw a romantic picture. We both love movies with romance. We saw a lot of kissing in that movie!

At last we went home. I cooked dinner and my cousin watched a late football game on TV! We enjoyed our dinner and went to bed! We didn't want to go anywhere or see anything else!

*Cassette users can have students listen to the script on tape.

B. Ask and answer the questions with your partner.

Pair students to do the exercise. Have them write down their own information first.

Lesson 14

How Was the Weather?

Communication Objectives:
>Report weekend activities
>Talk about the weather

New Structures:
>Past of *be*

Visuals:

V102	It's cloudy.
V103	It's sunny.
V104	It's windy.
V105	It's calm.
V106	It's foggy.
V107	It's clear.
V108	It's rainy.
V109	It's snowy.
V110	Let's Talk: Where Were You Last Weekend?

Page 124

✔ Review: Fun Outings

Do the review exercise in pairs, groups, or as a class.

Something New: How Was the Weather?

1. Ask "How's the weather today?" Hold up V102 and say "It's cloudy."

2. Repeat "It's cloudy" and have students repeat.

3. Follow the same procedure with V103–V109.

4. Review all eight visuals.

Page 125

☛ Practice: "It's windy"

Have students practice the conversations in pairs. Note both *information (how)* and *yes/no* questions.

Let's Talk: Where Were You Last Weekend?*

1. Show the visual to establish the context of the conversation: Sue and May are talking about last weekend.

2. Model the dialogue as students listen, indicating the speakers by pointing to the visual or other means.

3. Model the dialogue again.

4. Model the dialogue and have class repeat.

5. Take one role and have class take the other role; then change roles.

6. Divide the class in half and have them take the two roles; then have them switch roles.

7. Have volunteers say the dialogue for the class.

 8. Have class open books and practice the dialogue in pairs.

*Cassette users can have the students listen to the dialogue first with books closed.

Page 126 ☞ **Practice: "I was at the movies"**

Have students practice the conversations in pairs.

☞ **Practice Activity: How was the weather?**

Have pairs of students ask and answer questions about where they were and how the weather was.

Page 127 ☞ **Practice Activity: Weather around the World**

1. Read the introduction to the class.

 2. Have students ask four classmates about their native countries' weather. They should fill in the chart using the questions above as a guide.

3. Have them share their answers with the class.

Page 128 **Reading:** The Weather Report*

1. Read the passage to the class as students follow along in their books. Explain expression *in trouble*.

2. Check comprehension by asking oral questions about the passage.

3. Have students read the passage on their own.

*Cassette users can have students listen to the Reading first with books closed, and then listen again and read along silently.

Discussion

Facilitate a discussion of weather reports using the questions as a guide.

Page 129   ✍ **Writing**

Have students fill in the blanks to complete the questions and answers.

✍✍ **More Writing**

1. These can be done for homework.

2. Students will write a weather report about yesterday's and today's weather.

3. The next day have them share their work.

Lesson 14 Activity Pages

Page 130   📼 *A. Look at the pictures.**

    1. Go over the directions.

    2. Read the script or play the tape.

      Script:
      Listen to the weather reports and circle the correct picture.

      1. It's clear and calm here in Los Angeles. It's a sunny day.

      2. It's 65 degrees in Ann Arbor today. Don't forget your jacket; it's very cloudy.

      3. Wow! The wind is up today in Chicago! Expect windy weather all weekend.

      4. Hello, New Orleans! Be careful driving this morning: it's very foggy out there.

      5. We've had a record amount of rain this week in Houston and the rainy weather is supposed to continue all night!

*Cassette users can have students listen to the script on tape.

Page 131

B. Look at this page, and your partner looks at E on page 133.

Pair students. One looks at B on page 131 and the other looks at E on page 133. They take turns asking and answering questions about the missing information. Gary is done as an example.

Page 132

C. Look at the information in B or E. Write the questions and answers.

Students will use their completed charts to do the exercise.

D. Look at the postcard from Sara to her friend.

Students will choose from the eight words given to complete the postcard.

Page 133

E. Talk to your partner.

See B.

Places to Visit in the U.S.

Communication Objectives:
>Identify famous places to visit
>Talk about past trips

New Structures:
>None

Visuals:
>V111   I went to San Francisco on my vacation.
>V112   She went to New York City on her vacation.
>V113   He went to Yellowstone National Park on his vacation.
>V114   We went to Yosemite National Park on our vacation.
>V115   They went to Washington D.C. on their vacation.
>V116   We went to the Grand Canyon on our vacation.

Other instructional aids: Map of the United States

Page 134

✔ Review: Talking about the Weather

Write a weather report on the chalkboard and discuss it with the class.

Something New: The United States

1. Show the map of the United States. Identify some famous states and cities. Identify the regions of the U.S. Identify some national parks.

2. Do the Discussion questions together with the class.

Page 135

Something New: U.S. Landmarks

1. Briefly explain the lesson objective: To talk about some famous places in the U.S.

2. Explain *landmark*. Give examples from around the world and have students do the same.

3. Tell the class you are going to show some pictures of places people went on their vacations.

4. Hold up V111. Say "I went to San Francisco (on my vacation)." Have students repeat "I went to San Francisco."

5. Hold up V112 and say "She went to New York City (on her vacation)." Have students repeat "She went to New York City."

6. Follow the same procedure for V113–V116. Be sure to use the correct subject pronoun and possessive adjective each time.

7. Review all six visuals.

☛ Practice: "They went to the Grand Canyon"

 1. Review which states the landmarks are in.

2. Have students practice the conversations in pairs.

Page 136 ## ★ Something Extra: What Did You Do There?

1. Have students look at their books while you read the text of what the people saw and did at the various landmarks.

2. Ask "What did they do at Yosemite?" "What did he do in Washington, D.C.?" "What did you do in San Francisco?" "What did you do in New York City?" "What did you do at the Grand Canyon?" "What did you do at Yellowstone?" Elicit correct responses.

☛ Practice Activity: Guess the vacation places

1. Pass out the visuals of vacation destinations to six students, and have them come forward one by one.

2. Have students follow the directions for the guessing game. Go over the sample yes/no questions, and have students suggest others (like the 20 questions game).

Page 137 ### ☛ Practice: "What did he do there?"

Have students practice the conversations in pairs. They can practice with the other visuals of places and corresponding activities from the Something New and Something Extra sections.

🔲 Reading: A School Composition*

1. Explain that this is Lisa's school composition.

2. Read the passage to the class.

3. Explain any new vocabulary.

4. Check comprehension by asking oral questions about the passage.

5. Have students read the passage on their own.

*Cassette users can have students listen to the Reading first with books closed, and then listen again and read along silently.

Page 138
Discussion

1. Have volunteers answer the questions orally.

2. Ask several students #5 and #6.

✐ Writing

Have students complete the statements for #1 and #2, and the questions for #3 and #4.

Page 139
★ Something Extra: Famous Places Around the World

1. Have volunteers talk about famous places in their countries.

2. Have volunteers read the conversation.

3. Discuss the conversation and answer the questions below it.

Lesson 15 Activity Pages

Page 140
A. Talk about the picture.
Have students look at the picture and discuss Sam's Hawaiian vacation. They should mention where he went, what he did, what he saw, and the weather.

B. Look at the picture and write the conversation.
Students will write Sam's part, answering the questions.

Page 141
C. Make questions from the statements.
Students will write questions using *Did you...?* from the statements given. Then they will ask several classmates these questions, and will write down the names of students who answer "yes."

Unit Five | Evaluation

Page 143 🖭 **I. Listening Comprehension***

      1. Go over the directions for Part I with students.

      2. Read each item of the script two times, at normal conversational speed.

           Script:

           1. We went to the park yesterday.

           2. They went to the art museum.

           3. The children saw the elephants there.

           4. It was foggy in San Francisco.

           5. It's warm today.

           6. He went to Washington, D.C.

           7. Was the weather cold in San Francisco?

           8. Did they go hiking in Yosemite?

      *Cassette users can have students listen to the script on the tape.

Page 144 **II. Reading and III. Writing**

      1. Go over the directions for Part II and III with students.

      2. Have class do these sections independently.

Evaluation Check

      1. Correct evaluation by having student volunteers write their answers on the board or an overhead transparency.

      2. Have class check their answers.

      3. Circulate to make sure students have checked their work accurately.

Lesson 16

A Great Buy?

Communication Objectives:
> Identify types of cars
> Talk about buying/selling a car
> Interpret car ads

New Structures:
> Questions with *What kind of*
> Verb phrase *can afford*

Visuals:

> V117   a 2–door
> V118   a 4–door
> V119   a compact
> V120   a full–size car
> V121   a station wagon
> V122   a van
> V123   a sports car
> V124   Let's Talk: What Kind of Trade–in Can I Get?

Other instructional aids: Car ads from the newspaper

Page 146

✔ Review: Vacations

Have students discuss the two topics in groups. Make a list on the board of local places to visit.

Something New: Passenger Cars

1. Briefly explain the lesson objective: To learn about types of passenger cars and about buying and selling a car.

2. Hold up V117 and say "It's a 2–door."

3. Ask "What is it?" Answer "It's a 2–door," and have students repeat.

4. Follow the same procedure with the other six visuals.

5. Review all seven types of cars.

Page 147   ☛ **Practice: "It's a 2–door"**

Have students practice the conversations in pairs. Be sure they understand the difference between "he needs" and "he wants."

Page 148   ## **Something New:** New or Used?

1. Have students look at the illustrations in the text while you read the story about Ricardo.

2. Explain the meaning of *trade–in* and ask what students think Ricardo should do.

3. Have students read the story.

Discussion

Continue the discussion, using questions #1–2 as a guide.

 Let's Talk: What Kind of Trade–in Can I Get?*

1. Show the visual and explain that Ricardo is now at the used car lot with a salesman.

2. Model the dialogue as students listen, indicating the speakers by drawing pictures on the chalkboard, or other means.

3. Model the dialogue again.

4. Model the dialogue and have class repeat.

5. Take one role and have class take the other role; then change roles.

6. Divide the class in half and have them take the two roles; then have them switch roles.

7. Have volunteers say the dialogue for the class.

 8. Have class open books and practice the dialogue in pairs.

*Cassette users can have students listen to the dialogue first with books closed.

Page 149   ☛ **Practice: "I'm looking for a used car"**

Have students practice the conversations in pairs.

■ **Interaction:** Trading in Cars

 Pairs of students will role play salesman and customer using the sample dialogue.

Something New: Buying a Used Car

Show the visual as a transparency on the overhead. Explain the two ads, the used car lot, and the bulletin board notice. Ask oral comprehension questions.

☛ Practice Activity: Ads for Cars

1. Explain the abbreviations to the class.

 2. Divide the class into groups of 4–5 students each. Have each group discuss the ads on page 151, and choose which car they like. (You might also distribute actual newspaper ads for them to look at.)

Reading: A Two–Car Family?*

1. Read the passage to the class as students follow along in their books.

2. Check comprehension by asking oral questions about the passage.

3. Have students read the passage on their own.

*Cassette users can have students listen to the Reading first with books closed, and then listen again and read along silently.

Discussion

Facilitate a discussion of two–car families, using the questions as a guide.

✍ Writing

1. Students will write classified ads using the information in the boxes. They need to use abbreviations and then set a price for each.

2. Students will fill in the blanks to complete the conversation.

Lesson 16 Activity Pages

  ### A. *Listen to the people talk about their lifestyles.**
1. Have students listen to the people's stories and check what kind of car they need.

2. Read the script or play the tape.

> **Script:**
> Listen to the people talk about their lifestyles. Decide what kind of car they need and make a check in the correct column.

1. My name's Lisa. I'm 24 and single. I have a good job and I live in an apartment. I don't pay a lot of money for rent, so I have a lot of money for a nice car. I'd like a small car with a lot of pizzazz! I like to drive so I want a car that's fun and drives well.

2. My name's Ben. I'm married and I have two children. I work hard, so I have enough money to buy a big car, but I want something that will carry more than people. I'd like something modern and fun to drive.

3. My name's Ricardo. I'm looking for a used car. I have a compact now, but it's too small. I have kids, but I don't have a lot of money to spend. I need a car that's in good condition and has more than two doors.

4. My name's Carla. I'm single, and I live in a studio apartment downtown. I work far from my home, so I need a car that isn't very expensive to drive. I don't need a big car, and I don't have enough money for a sports car.

5. My name's Frances. I don't like to drive, but I drive every day. I'd like a car that's big and comfortable. My husband and I both work, so we have money for a big car. We have three kids and a dog, so we need a car we can take our whole family in.

6. My name's Magda. My husband and I don't have any children. We were married last month! But we do need a new car. We both work and I'm tired of taking the bus. His compact isn't running well, and we can't buy a sports car; they're too expensive. We need something nice, and not too expensive.

3. There may be some discussion about which car is best for each person. Explain that more than one answer may be correct, and ask students to explain their choices.

*Cassette users can have students listen to the script from the tape.

B. Read the advertisements and choose the car you'd like.
This is self–explanatory.

Page 154 **C. Ask and answer the questions about the advertisements on page 153.**
Students need to look at the four ads to do the exercise.

D. Write a short paragraph about the kind of car you would like to buy and why.
Students can do the last part for homework. They will write a short paragraph about buying a car. Have volunteers read their paragraphs the next day.

Delta's Apple Pie, Teacher's Guide 2A

We Bought It for Work and Play

Communication Objectives:
    Identify commercial vehicles
    Discuss public transportation
    Read about auto insurance

New Structures:
    Time expressions with *ago*

Visuals:
    V125 pick–up truck and truck and trailer
    V126 delivery van and taxicab
    V127 camper and trailer
    V128 jeep and motorcycle
    V129 Let's Talk: We Bought It for Work and for Play

Page 156

✔ Review: Buying and Selling a Car

1. Have students work in pairs to roleplay buying or selling a car.

2. After that, have the pairs write a classified ad to sell a car.

Something New: Vehicles on the Road

1. Briefly explain the lesson objective: To learn about commercial and recreational vehicles. Explain those two terms.

2. Explain that the first four items are vehicles on the job. Hold–up V125 and say "It's a pick–up truck." Have students repeat "pick–up truck." Repeat for "truck and trailer."

3. Follow the same procedure for V126.

4. Explain that the next four items are recreational vehicles. Hold up V127 and say "It's a camper." Have students repeat "camper." Repeat for "trailer."

5. Follow the same procedure for V128.

6. Point to the eight vehicles randomly and have students tell you what each is, and whether it's a commercial or recreational vehicle.

Let's Talk: We Bought It for Work and for Play*

1. Show the visual to establish the context of the conversation: Victor and Ken are talking about Ken's new pick–up truck.

2. Model the dialogue as students listen, indicating the speakers by pointing to the visual or other means.

3. Model the dialogue again.

4. Model the dialogue and have class repeat.

5. Take one role and have class take the other role; then change roles.

6. Divide the class in half and have them take the two roles; then have them switch roles.

7. Have volunteers say the dialogue for the class.

 8. Have class open books and practice the dialogue in pairs.

*Cassette users can have the students listen to the dialogue first with books closed.

☛ **Practice: "When did you buy it?"**

Have students practice the conversations in pairs.

Something Extra: Public Transportation

1. Read the introduction to the class. Explain *get around*.

2. Introduce the modes of transportation in the lesson and have class repeat each. Explain the differences.

3. Discuss which of the modes are available in your area.

☛ **Practice: "How do you get to work?"**

1. Explain *take* plus mode of transportation.

2. Have students practice the conversations in pairs. They can substitute different modes of transportation.

■ **Interaction:** Getting Around

 1. Divide the class into groups of four. Go over the directions and then have the groups do the exercise.

2. Have one member of each group report their findings to the class.

Reading: Auto Insurance*

1. Read the passage to the class as students follow along in their books. Explain new vocabulary.

2. Check comprehension by asking oral questions about the passage.

3. Have students read the passage on their own.

*Cassette users can have students listen to the Reading first with books closed, and then listen again and read along silently.

Page 160

Discussion

Facilitate a discussion of auto insurance using the questions as a guide.

✍ Writing

1. Students will write the appropriate question or answer for each item.

2. Students must choose from the words in the box to complete the cloze passage.

Lesson 17 Activity Pages

Page 162 **A. Listen to the people talk about the vehicles they use at work and at play.***

1. Students will listen and circle the correct picture for each item they hear.

2. Read the script or play the tape.

Script:
1. I drive around the city in my cab all day long. It's interesting work and I make good money driving a taxi.

2. I work for Flora's Floral Service. I deliver flowers for weddings and graduations. It's a nice job. People smile when they see me pull up in my van.

3. I don't have a job outside the home, but boy, do I work! I take six kids to school every other morning. My kids have classes every afternoon. Julia has ballet, Suzana has soccer, and there are always birthday parties or soccer games on the weekends. It's a good thing we have our wagon.

4. Our family loves to go camping in the national parks. It isn't very expensive, and it's a great way to take a vacation. Yes sir-ree, we bought a used camper last year, and we always drive our camper to our favorite site and have a great time!

5. I'm a contractor. I work with a construction company and supervise the construction of different buildings. I need a lot of tools, and usually I bring wood, or bricks, or other heavy things to a construction site. The company bought me a pick–up truck last month. My pick–up wasn't doing too well and so the company bought a new one. It's great to have a new truck.

6. My wife and I both work with computers. We both have good jobs and we make good salaries. Last year we got a great new car; it's a jeep. We drive it to work, and we drive it on the weekends. It's a lot of fun, and very practical in bad weather!

*Cassette users can have students listen to the script on tape.

Page 163 **B. Make questions from the statements.**
Students will write questions using *you* from the statements given. Questions are in both present and past tenses. They will ask several class-mates the questions, and then will write down the names of students who answer *yes*.

C. Talk about the picture.
Students will discuss how the people in the picture get to work and/or school.

Page 164 **D. Look at the picture and write the missing words in the story below.**
Students will choose from the words in the box to complete the cloze passage based on the picture from Exercise C.

Lesson 18

Driver Occupations

Communication Objectives:
>Identify driving occupations
>Ask/answer interview questions
>Talk about job requirements
>Talk about skills and experience

New Structures:
>*What do you do?* to ask about occupations

Visuals:
>V130   taxicab driver
>V131   bus driver
>V132   delivery van driver
>V133   delivery truck driver
>V134   bicycle messenger
>V135   heavy rig (semi) operator
>V136   Let's Talk: Do You Have a Good Driving Record?

Page 166

✔ Review: Vehicles on the Road

Follow the instructions given in the student text. Have volunteers do the writing on the chalkboard.

Something New: Driver Occupations

1. Briefly explain the lesson objective: To learn about different driving jobs and to interview for a job.

2. Ask "What's his occupation?" or "What's her occupation?" Hold up V130 and say "He's a taxicab driver." Have students repeat "taxicab driver."

3. Follow the same procedure with V131, V132, V133, V134 and V135.

4. Optional: Use the present tense to describe the jobs.
>Example: He's a taxicab driver—he drives a taxicab.

☛ **Practice: "What does he drive?"**

1. Explain that *What do you do?* is the same as *What's your occupation?*

2. Have students practice the conversations in pairs.

  Let's Talk: Do You Have a Good Driving Record?*

1. Show the visual to establish the context of the conversation: Rheza is applying for a job as a taxicab driver.

2. Model the dialogue as students listen, indicating the speakers by pointing or other means.

3. Model the dialogue again.

4. Model the dialogue and have class repeat.

5. Take one role and have class take the other role; then change roles.

6. Divide the class in half and have them take the two roles; then have them switch roles.

7. Have volunteers say the dialogue for the class.

 8. Have class open books and practice the dialogue in pairs.

*Cassette users can have the students listen to the dialogue first with books closed.

☛ **Practice: "Do you have experience?"**

1. Explain that the question *Do you have experience as a...* sometimes has the past tense as part of the answer.

2. Have students practice the conversations in pairs.

★ **Something Extra:** Auto Insurance Rates

1. Read the brief passage and explain *rates*.

2. Facilitate a discussion of auto insurance: The laws in your state, the importance of having insurance, the rate structure, etc.

★ **Something Extra:** Applying for a Job

1. Explain the chart. Ask questions such as "What's his occupation?" "What can he do?" "Does he have experience?" and elicit responses.

2. Have students ask each other these questions.

Page 170

■ Interaction: What Can You Do?

1. Have students draw the same chart on their own paper.

 2. They will walk around the room and ask their classmates the questions above in order to fill in the grid as directed in the text.

🔲 Reading: Men, Women and Jobs*

1. Read the passage to the class as students follow along in their books.

2. Check comprehension by asking oral questions about the passage.

3. Have students read the passage on their own.

*Cassette users can have students listen to the Reading first with books closed, and then listen again and read along silently.

Page 171

Discussion

Facilitate a discussion of men's and women's roles in society using the questions as a guide.

✍ Writing

1. Have students fill in the blanks to complete each item.

2. Below that, students will fill out a grid as before, but with information about themselves instead.

Lesson 18 Activity Pages

Page 172

A. Match the statement with the correct occupation.
Have students do the exercise as directed.

B. Look at the application form and answer the questions.
1. Go over the information given for Rafael.

2. Have students read and answer the questions below on their own.

Page 173

C. Fill out the application form with your information.
Have students do the exercise as directed—this time using their own information.

Unit Six Evaluation

Page 175 **I. Listening Comprehension***

1. Go over the directions for Part I with students.

2. Read each item of the script two times, at normal conversational speed.

Script:
1. It's a passenger car.

2. Ricardo is looking for a compact car.

3. She takes the bus to work.

4. He's a cab driver.

5. He has a good driving record.

6. They bought a camper.

7. Is he a delivery person?

8. What did she drive at her last job?

*Cassette users can have students listen to the script on the tape.

Page 176 **II. Reading and III. Writing**

1. Go over the directions for Part II and III with students.

2. Have class do these sections independently.

Evaluation Check

1. Correct evaluation by having student volunteers write their answers on the board or an overhead transparency.

2. Have class check their answers.

3. Circulate to make sure students have checked their work accurately.

Would You Like to Try It On?

Communication Objectives:
> Identify clothing sizes
> Discuss sale prices
> Read about mail order shopping
> Fill out an order form

New Structures:
> None

Visuals:
> V137 a (women's) small
> V138 a (women's) medium
> V139 a (women's) large
> V140 a (men's) small
> V141 a (men's) medium
> V142 a (men's) large
> V143 a (men's) extra large
> V144 Let's Talk: Would You Like to Try It On?

Other instructional aids: Examples of different colors

Page 178

✔ Review: Driver Occupations

Do the Review exercise as directed in the text.

Something New: Clothing Sizes

1. Briefly state the lesson objective: To learn about shopping for clothing.

2. Write the size abbreviations on the chalkboard. Explain that you are first talking about women's sizes, using a cardigan as an example.

3. Show V137, point to the abbreviation on the board, and say "It's a small." Have students repeat "It's a small."

4. Follow the same precedure for medium and large.

5. Explain that you are now talking about men's sizes, using a pullover as an example.

6. Show V140 and say "It's a small." Have students repeat "It's a small."

7. Follow the same procedure for medium, large, and extra large.

8. Review all the visuals and corresponding sizes.

Page 179   ☛ **Practice: "It's a large (size)"**

1. Review colors.

2. Have students practice the conversations in pairs.

🔊 **Let's Talk:** Would You Like to Try It On?*

1. Show the visual to establish the context of the conversation: Sue is shopping for clothes. She is at the sweater counter.

2. Model the dialogue as students listen, indicating the speakers by pointing to the visual or other means.

3. Model the dialogue again.

4. Model the dialogue and have class repeat.

5. Take one role and have class take the other role; then change roles.

6. Divide the class in half and have them take the two roles; then have them switch roles.

7. Have volunteers say the dialogue for the class.

 8. Have class open books and practice the dialogue in pairs.

*Cassette users can have the students listen to the dialogue first with books closed.

☛ **Practice: "A small in black, please"**

1. Explain the question *"How does it fit?"*

2. Have students practice the conversations in pairs.

Page 180   ■ **Interaction:** Buying and Selling

 1. Divide the class into groups of 4–5 students.

2. Supply real sweaters or use visuals V137–V143.

3. Follow the exercise as directed in the text.

Page 181
★ Something Extra: A T–Shirt Sale

1. Explain that you will be discussing sales. Show the visual as a transparency on the overhead.

2. Explain any new vocabulary (solids, stripes).

3. Ask comprehension questions about colors, prices (is/are, was/were), days of the sale.

Page 182
☞ Practice: "What's on sale?"

Have students practice the conversations in pairs.

■ Interaction: How Much Did You Save?

 1. Divide the class into small groups.

2. Read the introduction to the activity.

3. Have groups discuss sales and discount shopping.

Page 183
📼 Reading: Mail Order Shopping*

1. Read the passage to the class as students follow along in their books. Explain any new vocabulary items.

2. Check comprehension by asking oral questions about the passage.

3. Have students read the passage on their own.

*Cassette users can have students listen to the Reading first with books closed, and then listen again and read along silently.

Discussion

Facilitate a discussion of mail order shopping using the questions as a guide.

Page 184
✍ Writing

1. Students will fill in the chart following the two examples given.

2. In the next part, students will fill in the blanks to complete the dialogues.

Page 185 **A. Look at the sweaters, listen to the saleswoman, and write the correct prices on the tags.***

Read the script or play the tape. (*Note: When prices are written out this indicates slower speech.*)

Script:

1. Oh no! Someone forgot to put the prices on these sweaters. Looks like I have another job! Okay, let's see. This women's acrylic sweater, size 32, is $15.00. Let me write that: Fifteen dollars.

2. All right, let's look at this extra large sweater; oh, this is a men's pullover. These are $50.00. A little expensive, aren't they? Fifty dollars.

3. And this medium men's pullover is on sale; it's only $16.00 today. Sixteen dollars. My husband would like this.

4. Hmm…I'm not sure about this women's cardigan. It's a 38, 100% cotton. Oh, yes, these sweaters are $26.00. Twenty–six dollars.

5. Now this men's cardigan is a small, and I believe it's $14.00. Yes, that's right, fourteen dollars.

6. Ah, the last one, a size 34 women's Shaker sweater. Oh, this is a nice sweater. It's $44.00. Forty–four dollars. I'd like one of these.

*Cassette users can have students listen to the script on tape.

B. Talk about the chart below with your partner.

Students will work in pairs, asking and answering questions orally about the chart. You may want to practice the questions they will need first. (For sample questions, see exercise C.)

Page 186 **C. Look at the chart on page 185 and write the questions and answers.**

Have students do the exercise as directed in the text, using the information from the previous speaking activity.

Do You Have a Receipt?

Communication Objectives:
Exchange or return purchases
Describe ill–fitting clothing

New Structures:
Too + adjective

Visuals:
V145   too small
V146   too big
V147   Let's Talk: Do You Have a Receipt?

Other instructional aids: Examples of receipts and/or credit slips

Page 188

✔ Review: Buying Clothing

Pairs of students will role play customer and salesclerk as they practice the examples given in the text.

Something New: Too Small or Too Big

1. Briefly explain the lesson objective: To talk about exchanging or returning clothing that doesn't fit.

2. Hold up V145 and say "too small." Have students repeat.

3. Hold up V146 and say "too big." Have students repeat.

4. Hold up V145 again and say "The T–shirt *is* too small. The pants *are* too small." Have students repeat.

5. Hold up V146 again and say "The T–shirt *is* too big. The pants *are* too big." Have students repeat.

6. Do the substitution drill given under the pictures. Explain *tight/loose* if necessary.

Let's Talk: Do You Have a Receipt?*

1. Show the visual to establish the context of the conversation: Maria is at the department store to exchange a shirt for her son. Explain *receipt* and show examples, if available.

2. Model the dialogue as students listen, indicating the speakers by pointing or other means.

3. Model the dialogue again.

4. Model the dialogue and have class repeat.

5. Take one role and have class take the other role; then change roles.

6. Divide the class in half and have them take the two roles; then have them switch roles.

7. Have volunteers say the dialogue for the class.

8. Have class open books and practice the dialogue in pairs.

*Cassette users can have the students listen to the dialogue first with books closed.

Page 190 ☞ **Practice: "It's too big for me"**

Have students practice the conversations in pairs, making sure they use singular and plural correctly, along with subject/verb agreement.

Page 191 ★ **Something Extra:** Store Policy

 1. Explain *policy* and give examples.

2. Show page 191 as a transparency on the overhead, if possible. Have volunteers read the short conversation.

3. Ask comprehension questions about the situation.

4. Ask students about their experiences regarding store policies.

Page 192 ☞ **Practice: "I want to exchange this sweater"**

1. Explain the differences among *refund, exchange, return,* and *credit.*

 2. Have students practice the conversations in pairs.

🔊 **Reading:** Sue Was Lucky*

1. Read the passage to the class as students follow along in their books.

2. Check comprehension by asking oral questions about the passage.

3. Have students read the passage on their own.

*Cassette users can have students listen to the Reading first with books closed, and then listen again and read along silently.

Discussion

Do the Discussion questions as a class.

Page 193   ## ✍ **Writing**

1. Students will choose one item each to fill in the blank next to the definitions.

2. Students will fill in the blanks to complete the dialogues.

Lesson 20 Activity Pages

Page 194 🔊 ***A. Listen to the customers complain about their new clothes. Circle the letter of the correct picture.****

Read the script or play the tape. Repeat as necessary.

Script:

1. Oh no! This skirt is too short! I'm embarrassed to go out of the dressing room. I can't wear this skirt; it's much too short.

2. Oh brother! These pants are much too big. My diet is working but I can't wear these pants. They're falling off of me; they're so big.

3. Mom! This shirt is too tight! I can't breathe in it! You bought this for me yesterday? It's much too tight!

4. Mom! This dress is too long. I can't walk in it. You have to take it back right away. I need a dress that fits, not one that's too long!

5. Ah, at last! Pants that fit! I'm so happy to find pants that fit just fine! What a relief.

*Cassette users can have students listen to the script on tape.

B. Listen to the customers try to return the items.*

> 1. Have students listen to whether the customers want a credit, refund, or even exchange and make a check under the correct column.
>
> 2. Read the script or play the tape.

> ### Script:
>
> 1. I have to return this skirt. It's much too short. I'd like you to credit my account. What? Oh yes, here's my credit card.
>
> 2. I need to return these pants. They're too big. Yes, I know, they're very nice pants. I'd like to do an even exchange for a smaller size. Here's my receipt.
>
> 3. I have to return this shirt that I bought for my son. He's growing like a weed! What? Oh, the shirt is too tight. Yes, I'd like a refund. Why? Oh, well there's a sale on T–shirts at a store down the street and I can use the refund to shop for him there.
>
> 4. I'd like to do an even exchange on this dress I bought for my daughter. It's too long and she needs a new dress right away. Where can I find something in the same color, but a little smaller?
>
> 5. I want to return these pants. Yes, they were a perfect fit, but I don't want to buy such a large size. I'm trying to diet, so I'd like you to give me a credit. I want to come back when my diet is over and buy a smaller size.

> *Cassette users can have students listen to the script on tape.

C. Talk with your partner.

> Pair students. One looks at Exercise C on page 195 and the other looks at Exercise F on page 197. They take turns asking and answering questions about the missing information.

D. Look at the pictures and put them in order.

E. Look at the pictures on page 196 and write the missing words in the story.

> Students will choose from the words in the box to complete the cloze passage. (This passage tells the story depicted in the pictures on page 196.)

F. Talk with your partner.

> See C.

They Feel a Little Tight

Communication Objectives:
> Identify types of shoes and sizes
> Ask about shoe repair
> Describe shoe repair problems

New Structures:
> Quantifier *a pair of*

Visuals:

V148	women's dress shoes size 6A
V149	women's work shoes size 6B
V150	women's athletic shoes size 6C
V151	men's dress shoes size 10A
V152	men's work shoes size 10B
V153	men's athletic shoes size 10C
V154	Let's Talk: They Feel a Little Tight

Page 198

✔ Review: Shopping Problems

1. Do the discussion about returning and/or exchanging clothing.

2. Write some of students' suggestions on the chalkboard.

Something New: Men's and Women's Shoes

1. Briefly state the lesson objective: To talk about shoe sizes and widths, and buying and repairing shoes.

2. Hold up V148, V149, and V150, and say that these are women's shoes. Show V148 and say "They're dress shoes." Have students repeat "They're dress shoes."

3. Still showing V148, say "They're size 6A." "They're narrow." Have students repeat "Narrow."

4. Follow the same procedure with V149 (6B–medium) and V150 (6C–wide).

5. Hold up V151, V152, and V153, and say that these are men's shoes. Show V151 and say "They're dress shoes." Have students repeat "They're dress shoes."

6. Still showing V151, say "They're size 10A. They're narrow." Have students repeat "Narrow."

7. Follow the same procedure with V152 (10B–medium) and V153 (10C–wide).

8. Review all the visuals, grouped by width (6A/10A, etc.)

Page 199 ☛ **Practice: "My shoes are 11B"**

Have students practice the conversations in pairs.

 Let's Talk: They Feel a Little Tight*

1. Show the visual to establish the context of the conversation: Tomas is trying on some work shoes.

2. Model the dialogue as students listen, indicating the speakers by pointing to the visual or other means.

3. Model the dialogue again.

4. Model the dialogue and have class repeat.

5. Take one role and have class take the other role; then change roles.

6. Divide the class in half and have them take the two roles; then have them switch roles.

7. Have volunteers say the dialogue for the class.

 8. Have class open books and practice the dialogue in pairs.

*Cassette users can have the students listen to the dialogue first with books closed.

☛ **Practice: "I need some work shoes"**

Have students practice the conversations in pairs.

Page 200 & 201 ★ **Something Extra:** Shoe Repair

 1. If possible, show the six scenes on a transparency.

 2. Go over the six situations, one at a time, making sure students understand the problem and repair solution for each one.

 3. Optional: Give the solution and have students tell you the problem.

Page 202 ☛ **Practice Activity: What's the matter with these shoes?**

 1. Have students look at the pictures and write their answers on their own.

 2. Have pairs share their answers.

Page 203 ■ **Interaction:** Shoe Repair

 1. Form groups of 4–5 students.

 2. Have students discuss shoe problems.

📼 **Reading:** Shoes for the Family*

 1. Read the passage to the class as students follow along in their books.

 2. Check comprehension by asking oral questions about the passage.

 3. Have students read the passage on their own.

 *Cassette users can have students listen to the Reading first with books closed, and then listen again and read along silently.

Discussion

 Have class answer the questions orally.

✍ **Writing**

 1. Students must write one word in each blank to complete the cloze passage.

 2. Students will write a short paragraph about shoes they recently bought. This can be done for homework.

Lesson 21 Activity Page

A. Match the sentences with the problems.

Students will read on their own and do the matching as stated.

B. Read the statements and make the questions.

1. Students will write the questions using "Do you...?"

 2. Then they will walk around, ask classmates the questions, and write the names of students who answer "yes."

Unit Seven **Evaluation**

Page 205 📼 *I. Listening Comprehension**

     1. Go over the directions for Part I with students.

     2. Read each item of the script two times, at normal conversational speed.

             Script:
             1. He takes a large size.

             2. That looks good on you.

             3. Please exchange this sweater.

             4. They're on sale.

             5. My heels are worn out.

             6. They're too long for him.

             7. Does it fit?

             8. Is it too big for her?

     *Cassette users can have students listen to the script on the tape.

Page 206 ***II. Reading and III. Writing***

     1. Go over the directions for Part II and III with students.

     2. Have class do these sections independently.

Evaluation Check

     1. Correct evaluation by having student volunteers write their answers on the board or an overhead transparency.

     2. Have class check their answers.

     3. Circulate to make sure students have checked their work accurately.

| # Lesson 22

I'm Going to Get a Haircut

Communication Objectives:

Discuss beauty and barber shop services

Talk about planned activities

New Structures:

Be going to future

Present progressive used as future

Visuals:

V155   haircut

V156   shampoo

V157   blow dry

V158   set

V159   permanent (perm)

V160   dye

V161   manicure

V162   pedicure

V163   Let's Talk: I'm Going to Get a Haircut

V164   moustache

V165   gel

V166   beard

V167   goatee

V168   clipper

V169   sideburns

V170   Let's Talk: My Wife's Going to Be There All Day

Page 208

✔ Review: Buying Shoes

Pairs of students will do the roleplay activities as directed in the text.

Something New: Beauty Shop Services

1. Briefly state the lesson objective: To learn about beauty shop services.

2. Explain that the first group of services is for women, although students will see later that they are also for men. If they mention this, tell them they will discuss that part later.

3. Hold up V155 and say "It's a haircut." Have students repeat "haircut."

4. Follow the same procedure with V156, V157, V158, V159, V160, V161, and V162. (Note: for V159, say "perm" for permanent.)

5. Ask women students the Discussion questions.

Let's Talk: I'm Going to Get a Haircut*

Page 209

1. Show the visual to establish the context of the conversation: It's Saturday, and May Lei and her husband Tom are making plans for the day.

2. Model the dialogue as students listen, indicating the speakers by pointing to the visual or other means.

3. Model the dialogue again.

4. Model the dialogue and have class repeat.

5. Take one role and have class take the other role; then change roles.

6. Divide the class in half and have them take the two roles; then have them switch roles.

7. Have volunteers say the dialogue for the class.

8. Have class open books and practice the dialogue in pairs.

*Cassette users can have the students listen to the dialogue first with books closed.

☞ Practice: "I'm going to need a perm next month"

1. Point out the future meaning of "going to" in the dialogue above.

2. Have students practice the beauty shop conversations in pairs.

Something New: Barber Shop Services

Page 210

1. Briefly explain the lesson objective: To learn about barber shop services.

2. As before, explain that these services are for men only (as will be obvious anyway).

3. Hold up V164 and say "It's a moustache." (He's going to have it trimmed.) Have students repeat "moustache."

4. Follow the same procedure with V165, V166, V167, V168, and V169.

5. Do the discussion questions with the whole class. Explain *radical haircut*.

Page 211 **Let's Talk:** My Wife's Going to Be There All Day*

 1. Show the visual to establish the context of the conversation: May Lei's husband, Tom, is at the barber shop, talking to the barber.

2. Follow the same procedure as in the previous Let's Talk dialogue for this lesson.

*Cassette users can have students listen to the dialogue first with books closed.

☞ Practice: "What are you going to do?"

1. Explain some of the colloquial expressions used in the sample conversations.

2. Make sure students understand use of *going to* for future.

3. Have students practice the conversations in pairs.

Page 212 ### ★ Something Extra: Where Are You Going Tomorrow?

1. Explain that *Where are you going?* or *What are you doing?* can be used to express future plans. Give examples.

2. Use the sample given in the text as an illustration.

☞ Practice: "I'm going jogging Saturday"

Have students practice the conversations in pairs.

Page 213 **Reading:** Times Change*

1. Read the passage to the class, as students follow along in their books.

2. Check comprehension by asking oral questions about the passage.

3. Have students read the passage on their own.

4. Lead a discussion about men and women using both beauty and barber shops.

*Cassette users can have students listen to the Reading first with books closed, and then listen again, and read along silently.

✍ Writing

Students will choose from the words in the box to complete the cloze passage.

Page 214 📼 **A. Listen to the customers tell the receptionist what they'd like.***

1. Students will listen and circle the correct picture for each item they hear.

2. Read the script or play the tape. Repeat the whole script as necessary.

Script:

1. I'd like to come in at 4. Do you have an opening? You do? Great. My hair is too long. I need a haircut. Oh, and can I have Barbara cut my hair? I can! Great! See you at 4.

2. I love the cut I got last week, but I have a big party tonight. Can I come in this afternoon for a wash and set? I can? Oh, that's wonderful. I love the way Linda sets my hair.

3. My nails are a disaster, I tell you. I simply must see Debi today. Can she give me a manicure? She can? What time? Okay, I understand, she's very good. I can wait for my manicure until 3.

4. I'd like to come in tomorrow in the afternoon. Is Linda available? Oh, good. My gray is beginning to show again; I need to get my hair tinted. Maybe I'll try to go red this time. Linda does such a good job tinting; I'm sure she can make my hair a beautiful shade of red.

5. Uh, I came in last week for a cut, but I didn't get my sideburns trimmed. My wife says I look strange with my hair short and my sideburns long. So when can I come in to get my sideburns trimmed? Right now? All right. See you in 10 minutes.

*Cassette users can have students listen to the script on the tape.

Page 215 **B. Look at yesterday's schedule for Alberta's Beauty Salon.**

Pairs of students will take turns asking and answering questions about the information in the chart. Explain that the operators' names are first names, but that the customers' names are last names, so students will need to add Mr. or Ms.

C. Look at the schedule above and write the questions and answers.

Students will use the same schedule above, but will write the answers and questions this time.

Special Occasions

Communication Objectives:
   Talk about special occasions
   Give/receive compliments

New Structures:
   None

Visuals:
   V171 birthday
   V172 wedding
   V173 wedding anniversary
   V174 retirement
   V175 bridal shower
   V176 baby shower
   V177 Let's Talk: Surprise!
   V178 Let's Talk: Let's Have a Baby Shower for Layne

Page 216

✔ Review: Beauty and Barber Shops

1. List and demonstrate (if possible) the services that a beauty and barber shop offer.

2. Have pairs of students role play customer and operator discussing various services.

Something New: Celebrations

1. Define *celebrations* and briefly state the lesson objective: To talk about special occasions.

2. Hold up V171 and say "It's a birthday." Have students repeat "birthday."

3. Follow the same procedure for V172, V173, V174, V175, and V176.

4. Review all six visuals and remind students that they are all things we celebrate.

Page 217 **Let's Talk:** Surprise!*

1. Show the visual to establish the context of the conversation: It's Mei's birthday and her classmates are having a surprise party for her.

2. Model the dialogue as students listen, indicating the speakers by pointing to the visual or other means.

3. Model the dialogue again.

4. Model the dialogue and have class repeat.

5. Divide the class in three groups and have them take the three roles (whole class will read "class"); then have them switch roles.

6. Have volunteers say the dialogue for the class.

 7. Have class open books, read the introduction, and practice the dialogue in triads.

*Cassette users can have the students listen to the dialogue first with books closed.

☛ Practice Activity: What can you say?

Go over the explanations with the class, along with the examples.

Page 218

★ Something Extra: Compliments

1. Explain *compliments*.

2. Go over the examples of giving and receiving compliments from the text. Explain that in addition to "Thank you," the students should add something related to the compliment given (as in the text examples).

3. Have pairs practice the conversations.

☛ Practice Activity: Giving and Receiving Compliments

 Have pairs of students practice giving and receiving compliments. Use the situations suggested in the text, and others if desired.

Let's Talk: Let's Have a Baby Shower for Layne*

1. Show the visual to establish the context of the conversation: Rosa and Maria are planning a baby shower for Layne. Explain *shower*, as in showering someone with gifts, as opposed to bathing.

2. Model the dialogue as students listen, indicating the speakers by pointing to the visual or other means.

3. Model the dialogue again.

4. Model the dialogue and have class repeat.

5. Take one role and have class take the other role; then change roles.

6. Divide the class in half and have them take the two roles; then have them switch roles.

7. Have volunteers say the dialogue for the class.

8. Have class open books and practice the dialogue in pairs.

*Cassette users can have the students listen to the dialogue first with books closed.

Page 219 ☛ **Practice: "What are you going to give her?"**

Have students practice the conversations in pairs.

Page 220 🔲 **Reading:** A Bridal Shower*

1. Read the passage to the class as students follow along in their books. Explain any new vocabulary items.

2. Check comprehension by asking oral questions about the passage.

3. Have students read the passage on their own.

*Cassette users can have students listen to the Reading first with books closed, and then listen again and read along silently.

Discussion

Facilitate a discussion of bridal showers using the questions in the text as a guide.

Page 221 ✎ **Writing**

Have students do as directed in the text. For #5, elicit several different responses.

Page 222 🔲 **A. Something special just happened to each of these women.***

1. Students will put the numbers 1–5 under the picture of the item they hear.

2. Read the script or play the tape.

Script:

1. Isn't she beautiful? I just had her last week. Her name is Victoria Angelina Holmes. I feel pretty great for a women who just had a baby.

2. I'm so excited! I got so many presents from all my friends, and my mom, and my dad! We had a big party and there were 14 candles on my cake. I love my birthday!

3. I can't wait to show John all the presents we got. When John and I move into our new home, after we get married, we'll have all the appliances we need. Of course, we probably don't need three toasters. We can return those, I'm sure. Wow, that was the best bridal shower I ever went to.

4. It was a very romantic party and I enjoyed every minute of it. Matthew and I celebrated our 50th wedding anniversary last night. I feel like a bride. We danced, and ate cake, and then, Matthew told everyone how much he loved me. I love that old man!

5. I can't believe that I worked for that company for thirty years. I loved my job, but I'm happy to retire. And that retirement party was terrific. They gave me this lovely watch, but the best gift was these tickets to Hawaii in my pocket. Hawaii! Wait until I tell my children!

*Cassette users can have students listen to the script on tape.

B. Draw a line from the compliment to the answer.
Students will do as directed in the text.

Page 223 **C. Label the "photos" below with the titles in the box. Have fun!**
Students should understand that these are sarcastic compliments and are meant as a joke.

D. Talk about the picture.

Students will discuss Max and Edie's 50th anniversary party, as depicted in the text.

E. Look at the picture above and complete the story.

Students will choose from the words in the box to complete the cloze passage.

F. Change the statements into questions.

1. Students will write the questions using "Did you…?"

 2. Then they will walk around and write the names of students who answer "yes."

Lesson 24

Greeting Cards

Communication Objectives:
  Discuss appropriate greeting cards
  Write greeting card and postcard messages

New Structures:
  Preposition of time *in*

Visuals:

  V179 Happy Birthday!
  V180 Best Wishes!
  V181 Congratulations!
  V182 Thank you
  V183 Get Well Soon!
  V184 In Sympathy
  V185 Happy Mother's Day!
  V186 Be My Valentine
  V187 Let's Talk: We're Going to Get Him a Card

Other instructional aids: Actual examples of greeting cards

Page 226
✔ Review: Special Occasions

1. Facilitate a class discussion in which you review the topics listed in the text.

2. Have students practice giving and receiving compliments.

Something New: Cards for Special Occasions

1. Briefly explain the lesson objectives: To talk about cards for special occasions.

2. Hold up V179 and say "Happy Birthday! It's a birthday card." Have students repeat "birthday card."

3. Hold up V180 and say "Best Wishes! It's a wedding card." Have students repeat "wedding card."

4. Continue in the same manner with V181, V182, V183, V184, V185, and V186, giving the greeting first, and then the generic card type.

5. Review the greetings and have class repeat. Give the greeting and elicit the kind of card it pertains to.

6. Optional: Show examples of actual greeting cards, and share their titles with the class.

Page 227 ## **Let's Talk:** We're Going to Get Him a Card*

1. Show the visual to establish the context of the conversation: Sara is telling the class about their classmate, Ben Lee, who had surgery.

2. Model the dialogue as students listen, indicating the speakers by pointing to the visual or other means.

3. Model the dialogue again.

4. Model the dialogue and have class repeat.

5. Divide the class in three groups and have them take the three roles; then have them switch roles.

6. Have volunteers say the dialogue for the class.

7. Have class open books and practice the dialogue in triads.

*Cassette users can have the students listen to the dialogue first with books closed.

☛ Practice: "He needs back surgery"

Page 228

Have students practice the conversations in pairs.

★ Something Extra: Messages

1. If possible, do the pages from the text as a transparency. If not, simply point as you explain that greeting cards have special messages inside.

2. Optional: Show examples of actual greeting cards again, but this time share their inside messages with the class.

■ Interaction: Messages

Page 230

1. Divide the class into groups of 4–5 students each.

2. Have each group do the activity as directed in the text.

3. Be sure to write students' messages on the chalkboard at the end of the activity.

📼 Reading: Having a Wonderful Time*

1. Read the passage to the class as students follow along in their books.

2. Check comprehension by asking oral questions about the passage.

3. Have students read the passage on their own.

*Cassette users can have students listen to the Reading first with books closed, and then listen again and read along silently.

Discussion

Facilitate a discussion of picture postcards, travel, and vacations using the questions as a guide.

Page 231
✍ Writing

Students will write an inside–the–card message for each situation given.

```
╔══════════════════════════════╗
║  Lesson 24 Activity Pages     ║
╚══════════════════════════════╝
```

Page 232
A. Read the situations and write the number next to the correct card.
Students will match the situation on the left to the appropriate card on the right.

Page 233
B. Look at the pictures. Tell the story with your partner.
Pair students. They will tell the story (in order) of the two bikers and what happened (or happens) to them.

Page 234
C. Look at the pictures and write the questions and answers.
Students will use the pictures from Exercise B to do as directed in the text.

Unit Eight Evaluation

Page 235 **I. Listening Comprehension***

1. Go over the directions for Part I with students.

2. Read each item of the script two times, at normal conversational speed.

Script:
1. She's getting a perm.

2. She fixes her own hair.

3. He's growing a beard.

4. Happy Birthday, Elena.

5. It's a wedding card.

6. It was a surprise baby shower.

7. Did she have her baby last week?

8. That's a beautiful scarf.

*Cassette users can have students listen to the script on the tape.

Page 236 **II. Reading and III. Writing**

1. Go over the directions for Part II and III with students.

2. Have class do these sections independently.

Evaluation Check

1. Correct evaluation by having student volunteers write their answers on the board or an overhead transparency.

2. Have class check their answers.

3. Circulate to make sure students have checked their work accurately.

Notes

Notes

Notes

Notes

Notes

Notes